J. FELTON COVINGTON, JR.

An Autobiographical Cookbook by

BETTY TALMADGE

with

Jean Robitscher and Carolyn Carter
Foreword by Rosalynn Carter

Illustrated by Lois Ellen Masterson

How to Cook a Pig
& Other
Back-to-the-Farm
Recipes

A Fireside Book
Published by Simon and Schuster

A FIRESIDE BOOK
PUBLISHED BY SIMON AND SCHUSTER
A DIVISION OF GULF & WESTERN CORPORATION
SIMON & SCHUSTER BUILDING
ROCKEFELLER CENTER
1230 AVENUE OF THE AMERICAS
NEW YORK, NEW YORK 10020

MANUFACTURED IN THE UNITED STATES OF AMERICA

1 2 3 4 5 6 7 8 9 10

LIBRARY OF CONGRESS CATALOGING IN PUBLICATION DATA

TALMADGE, BETTY.
    HOW TO COOK A PIG & OTHER BACK-TO-THE-FARM RECIPES.

    INCLUDES INDEX.
        1. COOKERY, AMERICAN—GEORGIA.   2. TALMADGE, BETTY.
I. ROBITSCHER, JEAN, JOINT AUTHOR.   II. CARTER, CAROLYN,
JOINT AUTHOR.   III. TITLE.
TX715.T15   641.5'975   77-8837
ISBN 0-671-22680-0
ISBN 0-671-24378-0 PBK.

To the old folks
who preserved the tradition of country cooking
and
To the young
who brought it back in style

Contents

Foreword

Betty and I have more in common than our experiences during the times we each held the position as Georgia's First Lady. We both like good, plain cooking. We don't entertain with lavish menus replete with gourmet dishes. We both like to have time to pursue other activities—in Betty's case, a successful career—and give our attention to family and politics.

How to Cook a Pig is more than a ham recipe book. It is a contribution to disseminating early American spirit and lore to those parts of the country that have not yet tasted Brunswick stew, cracklin' bread and grits with red-eye gravy.

Here, in this book, Betty shares with us the kind of cooking we have always had, the kind to which others who strayed away from the simple ways our forebears prepared food are now returning. Along with party menus and family recipes, Betty shares herself— her whimsical accounts of business adventures and her devotion to the cause of women, always urging others like herself to find a pursuit of happiness "after the dishes are done."

ROSALYNN CARTER

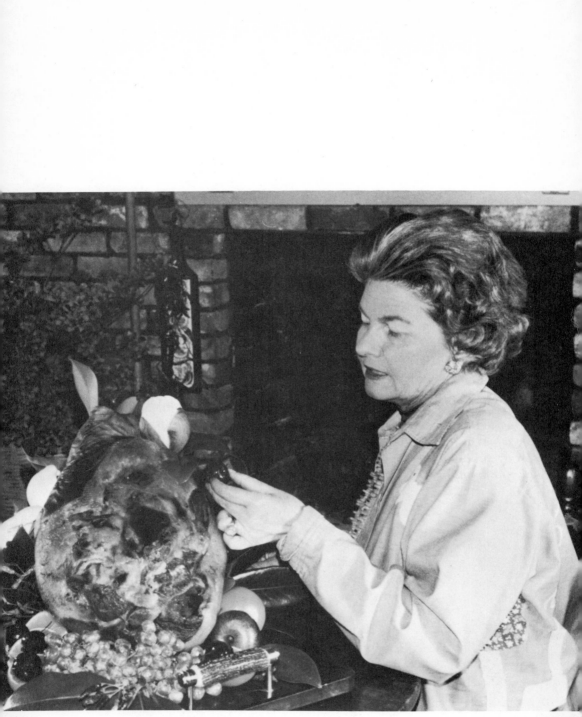

CAROLYN CART

Introduction

Food for Thought About Ham History

Nobody ever thought I'd write a cookbook—least of all, me. But I've been asked for years:

"How do you cook a ham?"

"How do you make country sausage?"

"What are your favorite recipes?"

"How did you get into the ham business?"

I guess I've rubbed a million hams in my time, and if you work with something long enough you're bound to pick up expertise.

My most prized possession is a trophy from my employees—a gold pig with this message engraved on the base: "Betty Shingler Talmadge—America's Greatest Pig Woman."

For years the Talmadge ham business was a small operation. Herman and I and a handful of workers saw that each ham had just the right formula of salt, spices and sugar rubbed into it. While the business was growing my employees had seen me working in every capacity as the unsalaried President, Secretary, Treasurer, Salesperson, Bookkeeper, Manager and Janitor! They thought I deserved recognition.

I'm happy to have a chance to answer some of the questions everyone has been asking. But I also want to share some of the stories and "pig lore" I've picked up along the way. I never felt I had a very scholarly approach to the ham business, so I've been doing some serious research to fill the gaps.

It was not surprising to me that honey was probably the first meat preservative. Honey just goes with ham. The Greeks and

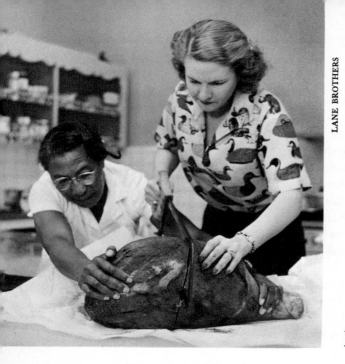

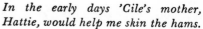

In the early days 'Cile's mother, Hattie, would help me skin the hams.

Romans used it to keep pork, which was more plentiful than beef, from spoiling, just as we use honey today to flavor ham in cooking.

John Drury's book about meats and meatmen tells about the honey jars of Greece and Rome that kept beef and pork from spoiling. He quotes from the world's oldest cookbook, written over two thousand years ago, a recipe to preserve cooked sides of pork and beef: "Place them in a pickle of mustard, vinegar, salt, and honey, covering meat entirely, and when ready to use—you'll be surprised!"*

I bet we'd be surprised if we tried that today.

In medieval days, salt and smoke, oil and vinegar were used to dry and preserve pork. Through the ages, people have sought ways to keep meat from spoiling. The expeditions of Marco Polo and later Christopher Columbus were as much in search of spices for preservatives as they were for riches.

Concern for preserving meats in this country came after the first settler realized that the wild deer and other game were becoming less plentiful, especially during the long winter months. They began dry-salting and brine-pickling pork, and they built smokehouses on their farms to cure the meat. They found that the smoke

* *Rare and Well Done, Some Historical Notes on Meats and Meatmen,* by John Drury, Quadrangle Books, Chicago, 1966, p. 28.

obtained from a low-burning fire of hickory or maple gave their meats the best flavor.

In my pursuit of knowledge I learned that back in the 1800s hogs were a bigger commodity than cotton in the South and worth nearly twice as much. The farmers had to get them to market on foot. A book recently published, *The Antebellum Southern Herdsman,* tells us how it was done.

The farmers would drive their herds of hogs from the Carolina uplands to marketplaces in Savannah, Charleston, Norfolk and even as far north as Philadelphia. A drive would sometimes include from three hundred to one thousand or more hogs with a "pigboy" for every hundred head and a manager for every herd. They could only be driven eight or ten miles a day.

So, where did they all spend the night?

In hog hotels, of course. I understand there were at least fifteen hog hotels on one fifty-five-mile stretch of road. The best known was at Alexander, ten miles north of Asheville, North Carolina, built around 1828 by Captain James Mitchell Alexander and carried on by his descendants for another half century. His hog hotel could accommodate four thousand hogs and fifty men at a time!*

Another part of hog heritage is now permanently recorded in Eliot Wigginton's *Foxfire* books. His students at the Rabun Gap-Nacoochee School of Georgia tell it like it is—or was, as the case might be.

When the students interviewed Bertha Dockins about her daddy's hog raising (wild hogs up in the mountains), she said that he would feed them a big sack of corn each week. When they

* "Hog Hotels Were Built for Mountain Drovers," column "Dateline Georgia" by Bob Harrell, *The Atlanta Constitution,* Oct. 1, 1975, excerpts from *The Antebellum Southern Herdsman: A Reinterpretation,* by Forrest McDonald and Grady McWhiney.

Actor-Senator George Murphy gets one of our early Talmadge hams.

LANE BROTHERS

CAROLYN CARTER

'Cile likes old-time cook-ing.

were fat enough, he'd sell most of them. But those he kept to cure went through this process:

Daddy'd pack his meat in a big old box, salt all over it, and let it stay there about two months, and he'd take it out then and wash it and hang it. Let drip from November to about March and he'd wash it and let it dry, and put it in any kind of a cotton sack, tie it up real good, and most of the time, just hang it back up.*

I remember from my own childhood down in Ashburn, Geor-gia, that the first cold snap put every member of the house into action. The hogs were slaughtered and the meat was prepared in a continuous work effort. The farm hands and household help, along with everyone in the family, would be involved in rendering lard (nibbling on the cracklin's as a reward!), or cutting the hams and slabs of bacon. Many would work all night.

I am so glad Eliot Wigginton is exposing our young people to the ways of the past—to some of the romance as well as the hard-ships of living without refrigeration and other conveniences.

Few people who have read the first *Foxfire* volume will ever for-get Aunt Arie's struggle trying to get an eyeball out of a fresh hog's head. When she did, she threw it out the back door. It landed on a nearby tin roof, rolled off and hung bobbing on the clothesline. Then she explained to the astonished students interviewing her that she was preparing the hog's head to make souse meat.

* *Foxfire 3,* edited by Eliot Wigginton, Anchor Press/Doubleday, New York, 1975, p. 111.

Her recipe:

I'll soak this now, and soak all th' blood out of it until in th' mornin' it's just as white. Then I'll take an' grind it on that sausage grinder an' take th' juice that it cooked in, part of it, and put some sage 'n' black pepper 'n' red pepper and stirr–r–r it all up until it's so good 'n' fine as it can be, and then put it in them cannin' jars 'n' seal it. Then open it in th' winter. I love it better'n anything in th' world. . . .*

Come to think of it, Aunt Arie's right. The eyes of the hog are about the only part you have to throw out. Almost everything else can be roasted, baked, ground, fried, pickled or canned, from the ears down to the hind feet! It is even possible to use the heart, lungs, liver and kidneys. Of course, the fat scraps can be cut up for lard. You can hardly find a better bargain in livestock.

Old-timers can give you lots of hog recipes—recipes for "pressed hog's head," hog's head stew, boiled tongue, scrambled eggs with hog brain, "liver mush," "lights" or boiled lungs, even roasted snout! They have ways for cooking everything but the eyeballs and the squeal!

One thing this research has done for me—when I'm thrown into intellectual circles in Washington or Atlanta or wherever, the one subject I can discuss with more scholarly knowledge than anyone else is How to Cook a Pig.

* *Foxfire 1*, pp. 20–22.

Even Yankee Adlai Stevenson learned something about country ham from me.

The ingredients for cooking this book: Carolyn Carter, yours truly, and Jean Robitscher.

HOW TO COOK A BOOK

I know one surefire recipe. It is How to Cook a Book: Find two good friends who are free-lance writers and fun to be around. Then share the work of putting it all together!

I grew up with Carolyn (McKenzie) Carter in Ashburn, Georgia, and have enjoyed watching her success as a writer and photographer. She has received the award Master of Photography, given by the profession, and her pictures and stories were published in the *Atlanta Constitution & Journal Sunday Magazine* for many years. Carolyn specializes in travel articles.

Jean (Begeman) Robitscher is a former Washington, D.C., columnist and writer. Jean and Liz Carpenter, who was Lady Bird Johnson's Press Secretary, once wrote a column together called "Southern Accents in Washington." Jean was an assistant editor of *The New Republic* in Washington, D.C., for many years, and co-author of *Learning Joy* (Whitmore Publishing Co., 1977) , and a juvenile textbook, *Notable Men and Women of the Civil War* (Precision Publishing Co., 1970). She is now a free-lance writer in Atlanta, Georgia.

BETTY TALMADGE

Editor's Note: Betty Talmadge, an expert on hams, is president of a meat sales organization, Betty Talmadge & Associates. For many years she has been a Washington hostess as wife of Georgia's United States Senator Herman Talmadge and was First Lady of Georgia during his two terms as Governor. She is rapidly becoming an "international entrepreneur," since she is now associated with Linder International and exports her meat products to Japan.

Our farm is "Gone With the Wind" vintage.

PART I

Parties Down on the Farm and Up in Washington

I'VE NEVER TRIED TO COMPETE with Washington's "hostess with the mostest" or "host with the most" (now that some men are competing for equal rights in the kitchen). Everyone seems to thrive on parties there, but even though I spend much of our time in the nation's capital, I would rather entertain down on the farm. I'm more at home in Lovejoy, Georgia.

I grew up in south Georgia, where my family, the Shinglers, owned a farm in Ashburn. After Herman served in World War Two as a naval officer, his father gave us an old worked-out farm near Lovejoy, about twenty-five miles south of Atlanta. The house was old and worked-out, too, so I set about fixing it up. It is a hundred-and-fifty-year-old farmhouse, and even though the rooms are only a comfortable size, we have entertained from twenty to seven hundred people from time to time, serving buffet style in the dining room and letting the folks eat standing up or sitting at tables and on the grass outside.

When people come to our house they expect country ham. The

few times when I've served something different they usually ask: "Where's the ham?"

So I've tried to perfect a menu that is a complement to country ham. We start with mint juleps; then our menu varies slightly depending on the time of day and time of year.

In winter, we often serve country ham, fried chicken, baked grits, candied apples, cucumber mousse with sliced tomatoes, green beans or turnip greens, 'Cile's corn bread, hot biscuits and pecan tassies.

In summer, for an informal luncheon or supper, we might have country ham, fried chicken, stewed fresh corn, cucumber mousse with tomatoes, candied apples, hot biscuits, and for dessert fresh peaches with lace cookies.

If you become accustomed to one menu and do it frequently, you feel comfortable with it. It enhances the meal to cut down on anxiety in preparing it. You should have the proper knives, pans, containers and serving dishes for your meal. This enables you to enjoy the party and the guests, too. Genuine hospitality is more important than the food.

I find it easy to entertain at Lovejoy. While the house is not large by today's standards, it was once considered a "plantation." You can't help but feel a sense of history, knowing that the house is located where Civil War military maneuvers took place over a century ago during the Atlanta Campaign. It was owned then by a prominent Confederate, Dr. George Gilmore Crawford. Some say the Hollywood scenes depicting rural Georgia in the movie *Gone With the Wind* show our house the way it looked before we renovated it, but I've never been sure.

In 1942, the estate of Miss Arie Crawford sold the plantation to Father Talmadge, who never occupied the house. It had been tenant-occupied from 1935 until we moved in twelve years later. The depression years, together with a decade of tenancy, had taken a heavy toll. It was a challenge to bring the old place back to life.

"Auntie Mame" at Lovejoy: A Hunt Breakfast

AT THE FARM, as in our apartment in Washington, most of our parties are small—a Sunday brunch for a few neighbors or a buffet supper for ten or twenty. But now and then we are called to greater efforts. My friends Liz Carpenter and Mrs. Lyndon B. Johnson once got me involved with the movie industry. Before I knew what was happening, I was giving a party for Lucille Ball and three hundred guests when she came to Atlanta to open her movie *Mame*. The proceeds were to benefit the LBJ Memorial Grove, and Lady Bird Johnson was the guest of honor along with Miss Ball.

Our old farmhouse with its white pillars and magnolia trees was a natural for the Hunt Breakfast. Although the dogwood and peach blossoms were out, the temperature dipped to 40° that day. We had asked some of our friends' daughters to shed their jeans and pose as Southern belles in costumes from Tara times and they stood shivering on the porch as they greeted the guests.

Miss Ball was shivering too as she rode in an open touring car, flanked by horsemen in red-and-black hunt costumes galloping up to the house. TV camera crews were everywhere. The place looked like a Hollywood setting for sure.

With their mint juleps in hand, guests filed through the dining room. The table was laden with country ham, sausage balls, baked cheese grits, Sally Lunn bread and beaten biscuits, bowls of strawberries and lace cookies.

Cold as it was, many guests took their plates outside, where we

Lucille Ball's theatrical entrance in an open Rolls-Royce gave the Hunt breakfast at the Talmadge farm a fantastic opening scene. Friends and entertainers gather to welcome her.

Having seen Mame *the night before, Lady Bird Johnson and I loved the chance to give the star a rave review. Former Secretary of State Dean Rusk gave the party an intellectual touch!*

had a Dixieland band playing tunes from *Mame*. There was a moment during that day when I felt misplaced in time. Could I really be entertaining a former First Lady and a famous star and her Hollywood entourage, along with my Atlanta friends—all having a ball down on the farm?

HUNT BREAKFAST

The Perfect Mint Julep
White House Scrambled Eggs
Country Ham
Sausage Patties
Baked Cheese Grits
Hot Biscuits
Sally Lunn Bread
Fresh Strawberries Laced with Bourbon
Lace Cookies

The Perfect Mint Julep

mint sprigs	*soda water*
1 teaspoon fine granulated sugar	*3 ounces bourbon*

For each julep, crack enough ice, very fine, to fill a collins glass almost to the top. Set the glass aside. Strip leaves from two sprigs of mint and muddle with sugar in another glass; then add a splash of soda water and the bourbon. Strain over the ice in the prepared glass and work a long-handled spoon up and down in the mixture until the outside begins to frost. Top with a splash of rum and a sprig of mint.

White House Scrambled Eggs
on Tomatoes

I don't know how many people have wangled a recipe out of White House Chef Henry Haller. Not many, I'm sure, so I'm proud to be one.

Betty Ford invited some 300 women who had helped her with the avalanche of mail following her mastectomy to an early-morning breakfast. Imagine serving scrambled eggs hot to that crowd. Most of us have trouble getting scrambled eggs from the range to the table in lukewarm condition every morning just for our family.

I had to have the recipe. So I called the White House the next morning and Chef Haller promised to send it to me. He did and I've used it many times since for our brunches at the farm.

First, make Hollandaise Sauce in a blender (p. 26).

Then make Basic Cream Sauce (p. 26).

Several hours before the guests arrive, cut medium-sized tomatoes in half, de-seed (so egg mixture will settle in when you add it later) and broil lightly.

Then break eggs into a bowl (allowing 1 large egg per person). Beat the eggs lightly. Combine 3 parts eggs to 1 part Basic Cream Sauce (I usually use a measuring cup and simply put in ¾ cup of eggs and ¼ cup of sauce). Scramble this mixture in a buttered frying pan to a soft consistency—barely firm enough to hold together when packed into an ice-cream scoop for individual servings.

Place 1 scoop of egg on top of each tomato half. (This can be done a couple of hours before guests arrive). Set aside at room temperature.

Just before serving, top each tomato-egg portion with a sauce of 2 parts hollandaise and 1 part cream sauce. Run under broiler until hot and bubbly. Garnish with fresh parsley and serve. If you are serving a large group, you can prepare several trays of these and keep them warm in the oven after broiling.

Blender Hollandaise Sauce
(*no cooking*)

3 *egg yolks*
1 *tablespoon lemon juice*

dash cayenne
¼ *pound butter*

Place egg yolks in blender with lemon juice and cayenne. Cover. Quickly turn blender on and off. Heat butter to almost boiling. Turn blender on high speed and slowly pour butter into mixture. Blend until thick and fluffy (about 30 seconds). Place sauce over warm—*not hot*—water until serving time. Makes about ⅔ cup.

Basic Cream Sauce

1 *tablespoon flour*
1 *tablespoon butter*
1 *cup hot milk*

heavy dash of Worcestershire
   sauce
salt and pepper

Blend butter with flour in top part of double boiler, directly over low heat, stirring constantly for a minute or two. Then add hot milk gradually, stirring. Place top of double boiler over hot water and cook 10 minutes, stirring frequently. Season to taste with Worcestershire sauce, salt and pepper.

For a heavy, thicker sauce, use 2 or 3 tablespoons flour and 2 tablespoons butter with 1 cup hot milk and follow same directions.

(Cream sauces can be used as a base for cream soups, for creaming vegetables, and in making soufflés and croquettes. So many recipes today call for a can of cream of chicken soup or a can of cream of mushroom soup. You can do these yourself with this basic cream sauce, chicken broth and/or a can of mushrooms.)

Talmadge Country-Cured Ham

Wash ham thoroughly. Place it in a large container or sink filled with lukewarm water and soak overnight.

Drain ham and place in roaster. Pour 2 pints of Coke or fruit juice and an equal amount of water over ham. Cover with lid or foil and bake at 350° F. approximately 20 minutes per pound. I usually bake a 15- or 16-pound ham at least 5 hours.

Remove outer skin from the ham and cut off excess fat. Score remaining fat in diamond shapes and insert whole cloves.

Combine 2 cups of brown sugar with 2 cups of pineapple juice and bring to a boil. Use this to baste the ham as it bakes for about 20 minutes more in a hot (450° F.) oven. Or use one of the more elegant glazes (see index).

Serve thinly sliced—slices should be no thicker than 1/4 inch—on a platter garnished with fruits. Before serving I sometimes decorate the ham with whole canned red crab apples, white grapes, preserved kumquats, pickled peaches or whatever fruit I happen to have. Or shave the ham into thin slices to put between biscuits.

Sausage Patties

From 1 pound of mild or hot country sausage, pinch off bits and press into patties 3/4 inch thick and 2 inches in diameter. Place patties on rack in shallow baking pan. Bake in 400° F. oven for 30 minutes. Yield: 8 patties.

These can be made in advance and refrigerated overnight (or frozen for a longer period) and rewarmed when ready to serve for a large party.

Baked Cheese Grits

There is no better recipe than this to make someone into a grits lover.

4 *cups water*
2 *teaspoons salt*
1 *cup grits (plain or speckled)*
2 *cups extra-sharp Cheddar cheese, grated*

1 *stick butter (or margarine)*
1/2 *teaspoon Worcestershire sauce*
4 *eggs, separated*
milk (only if necessary)

Bring salted water to a boil. Add grits gradually. Reduce heat and cook until mixture becomes thick, stirring frequently, about 20 to 30 minutes. Add 1½ cups of the cheese, the butter and Worcestershire sauce while hot and set aside. Beat egg yolks and add. If grits are too stiff, add milk to make them medium soft.

Grease shallow 1½-quart casserole with butter. Beat egg whites until stiff and fold into grits. Pour grits into casserole, top with remaining ½ cup cheese. Bake at 350° F. for 35 minutes. Serves 6 to 8.

'Cile's Biscuits

'Cile is Lucille Kelly, who has reigned over our kitchen for many years. We cooperate when we have a party, each cooking our specialties. The recipes with her name are those I wouldn't think of doing if she is around. 'Cile says of these biscuits, "Don't fool around with the dough. Make them quickly and bake them quickly for best results."

2 cups all-purpose flour	*4 tablespoons shortening*
4 teaspoons baking powder	*⅔ cup milk*
1 teaspoon salt	

Sift flour, baking powder and salt into bowl. Cut shortening into mixture until it forms tiny balls. Add milk and stir quickly with a fork until you have a soft dough.

Knead dough quickly on floured board. Pinch off enough to make small balls, roll them in hand and flatten into discs about ¼ inch in diameter. Place on cookie sheet. Bake at 500° F. for 10 minutes. Yield: about 25 biscuits.

Louise Hastings' Sally Lunn Bread

Truly a good neighbor, Louise always makes this for me when I entertain. It is delicious and worth the time it takes to prepare.

1 cup lard	*2 eggs*
½ cup sugar	*2 yeast cakes*
1 cup boiling water	*1 cup lukewarm water*

6 cups unsifted flour	1 teaspoon baking soda
1 teaspoon baking powder	1 teaspoon salt

Cream lard and sugar; add boiling water; *cool*. Dissolve yeast cakes in lukewarm water, add to lard-and-sugar mixture. Add eggs, beaten slightly. Sift together flour, baking powder, soda and salt. Add to above.

Keep overnight in the refrigerator. Next day, divide dough and place in 2 greased loaf-cake pans. Butter tops of the loaves. Bake in 350° F. oven until done, approximately 30 minutes. Yield: 16 servings.

Fresh Strawberries Laced with Bourbon

Leave stems on strawberries and wash them thoroughly. Pile the strawberries high in a large glass bowl or on a serving platter. Have handy a little bowl of bourbon next to a bowl of powdered sugar—the combination makes a delicious dip for the strawberries.

Lace Cookies

These delicate cookies have a Southern touch.

2¼ cups regular oatmeal	1 cup butter, melted
2¼ cups light-brown sugar	1 egg
3 tablespoons flour	1 teaspoon vanilla
1 teaspoon salt	

Lightly mix the oatmeal, sugar, flour, and salt in a bowl; do not use an electric mixer. Add the melted butter and stir. Add slightly beaten egg and vanilla; mix well.

Grease a sheet of heavy aluminum foil or a cookie sheet. From the end of a teaspoon, drop small quarter-size circles onto the foil or baking sheet. Bake 8 to 10 minutes in a 350° F. preheated oven.

2

Roast Pig, Georgia Style: Politickin' and Pig-Pickin'

THERE IS A FAMOUS ESSAY called "A Dissertation Upon Roast Pig" by the English essayist Charles Lamb that preserves the earliest recipe on how to cook a pig: Burn down your house with your pig in it.

As the story goes, a young country boy in China accidentally burned down his father's house where the family had kept nine suckling pigs. He got into a lot of trouble because he tasted one of those delicious little roasted pigs. In ancient China eating "burnt" flesh was a crime, so until that event no one had ever tasted cooked meat. The burned-down house was held to be an extenuating circumstance, however. The word spread on how good burnt pig tasted, and the story recounts the sight of villagers burning their homes to be able to eat burnt pig without being arrested! The story ends with the discovery that all meat might be cooked without first burning down a house, and instead, by using a "rude form of a gridiron. . . ."

Now the "gridiron" method is something I can tell about when it comes to roasting pig. We call it a "pig-pickin'" in Georgia. This will be my own Dissertation Upon Roast Pig—Georgia style!

You have to plan ahead for a pig-pickin' party. A pig-roasting, pit or grill style, can keep our house in an uproar for several days. But it's worth it because the whole family joins in the fun.

For as long as I can remember, politickin' and pig-pickin' have gone together. Whenever candidates stump their districts or the state, barbecues are held on the courthouse squares of almost every county seat in Georgia. I've been to hundreds.

The Carter campaign gave me the opportunity to have one of the biggest pig-pickin' parties Georgia has seen in a long time. The women in the Democratic Party wanted to honor Rosalynn Carter and Joan Mondale, who had campaigned so feverishly and effectively around the country. It was the last month of the campaign and we had only a week to get the whole plan in motion. With the help of loyal Democrats, friends and the weather, we had nearly five hundred guests at our pig-pickin'.

The theme of the fund-raiser was "51.3%," which represents the total percentage of women in the United States population, so everyone who came, including a lot of men, donated $51.30 for a platter of country food. United States Representative Lindy Boggs (D., La.), who was our headwoman to introduce the dignitaries, welcomed the crowd and told the women she was glad they had brought their "lovely, attractive, helpful, efficient husbands."

Although I had to have some of the food brought in by professionals, we did much of the cooking ourselves in advance. We multiplied my favorite Cheese Grits recipe by thirty, renamed it "Fritz's Grits" for the day, and everyone there with a camera photographed Joan eating it.

Two of my Jonesboro neighbors, Blanche Ledford and Anita Maddox, cleared their schedules and made four hundred Pecan Tassies. Other friends made an additional five hundred. They freeze well, so we were able to have nine hundred ready on the day of the pig-pickin'.

Louise Hastings decorated two whole barbecued pigs for the center of the serving tables. She surrounded each with magnolia leaves and seed pods, clusters of slender orange peppers and pale-pink plumed cockscomb, plus large green, orange and white Turk's-cap squash. The squash and leaves were also used to decorate all the tables covered with red cloths that were set up under shade trees and under a tent we had rented for the occasion.

We had forty-two gallons of Mama's Brunswick Stew, which we served in an old iron washpot with a long-handled soup dipper. The guests consumed seven barbecued pigs, eight gallons of watermelon-rind pickles, another eight of mixed sweet pickles, forty pounds of coleslaw and six hundred slabs of 'Cile's Corn Bread. We even had a lemonade stand that advertised "Amy's Lemonade" and was run by a steady stream of children from everywhere who had come to see the fun.

That's what a pig-pickin' is all about—just plain fun.

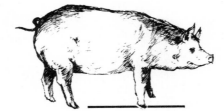

PIG-PICKIN' PARTY

Whole Roast Pig
Ocilla Coleslaw
'Cile's Corn Bread
Mama's Brunswick Stew
Chitlins
Barbecued Ham and Shoulders
Barbecue Sauce
'Cile's Candied Apples
Crusty Sweet Potato Casserole
Grandmother Shingler's Liver Pudding
Kitty Brewster's Pickles
Pecan Tassies

CAROLYN CARTER

Photos taken at two pig-pickin' events down on the farm show that roast pig—Georgia style—is always the center of attention. At the pig-pickin' for Rosalynn Carter, Amy's lemonade stand did a brisk business.

Pig-pickin' and politickin' are inseparable in Georgia. Here Herman greets Rosalynn, and Joan Mondale has her first taste of Fritz's Grits. Louise Hastings remained her calm and lovely self arranging my centerpiece for the festive day.

Whole Roast Pig

To roast a 20- to 40-pound pig in an outdoor pit or on a grill takes plenty of preparation and patience, along with the prospect of elaborate praise from family and friends. I prefer to keep the whole operation out-of-doors. The true smoked flavor can't be matched and the preparation is worth the effort. Here is my method:

1. Wash the pig, which has been split open and cleaned by a butcher. Marinate it overnight or for several hours in a mixture of lemon juice and garlic—several crushed cloves of garlic in about ½ gallon of lemon juice. Turn pig in marinade 2 or 3 times. Remove from marinade.

2. Rub the pig inside and out with about 1 cup of salt. Place washed river rocks or stones in the body cavity to help retain the shape of the pig's body. (Put a rock in the pig's mouth so an apple will fit there later.) Stitch the cavity closed with string or wire.

3. Light the coals in the pit or grill. I use a converted oil drum which has a gas burner under the coals and can keep a steady 200° F. to 250° F. temperature during the long cooking process.

4. Insert a thermometer in a fleshy part of the pig, making sure it doesn't touch bone. When ready to roast, place the pig on the hot grill and puncture the skin in 10 to 15 places with a sharp knife so the fat will be able to drip during the cooking process. The skin will split if you don't. Baste with marinade about once an hour, each time puncturing the skin with the knife to keep the fat dripping and to allow the marinade to penetrate.

5. After 1 hour, cover the ears and tail with damp cloths. Dampen the cloths every hour as the pig cooks to keep the ears and tail from burning. A 30- or 40-pound pig will take from 12 to 14 hours' cooking time. Be sure the internal temperature reaches 170° F. before you consider the pig done.

6. Remove pig from grill to a large wooden slab or serving platter and decorate. Decorating the pig is part of the fun. Let your imagination run wild. Put an apple in its mouth and use an olive for each eye. Use grapes, apples, pomegranates, squash, peppers or anything else that's attractive and available, plus some magnolia or other leaves to form a bed when it is brought to the table.

Carving the pig is somewhat of an art. When I'm having a party, I usually cook one ahead to leave intact for the serving buffet centerpiece and carve the other in the kitchen. The one on the table can be frozen after the party. Before freezing I cut the meat from the bones and freeze it in portions of various weights for family and party use.

Roast pig can be served with a variety of sauces: tomato, barbecue, fruit or other combinations. Then guests can eat the pork plain or choose from the sauces, which should be served piping hot.

Pig-picking' parties call for informal decor. I like to use tin mugs for the cold mint juleps and bloody Marys we serve on the back terrace. Each table, covered with a red-and-white-checked cloth, has as a centerpiece a clay pot with leaves and flowers from the garden. We usually serve about 50.

Ocilla Coleslaw

Ocilla is a small Georgia town best known for its annual Sweet Potato Festival as well as its Coleslaw.

1 cup corn oil
1 cup sugar
1 cup apple cider vinegar
2 teaspoons celery seed
2 teaspoons powdered mustard
   salt and pepper to taste

1 large cabbage, coarsely
   shredded
1 large onion, sliced in rings
2 green peppers—chop coarsely

Combine corn oil, sugar and vinegar and boil slowly for 5 minutes in an enamel or stainless steel saucepan. Add celery seed, mustard, salt and pepper. Cool slightly.

Combine cabbage, onion and peppers with marinade in a glass or china bowl and let stand in refrigerator for 24 hours. Serves 20 or more.

'Cile's Corn Bread

I never make the corn bread—that is 'Cile's department. When anyone asks for the recipe, she says, "I don't measure —I just make it!" Here are the ingredients and, I hope, the measurements. Use plain *cornmeal (not self-rising).*

2 cups cornmeal	1 teaspoon salt
1 teaspoon sugar	1 tablespoon shortening

Sift dry ingredients. Work in shortening. "Run water to get it real warm and then add just enough so it sticks together." Pinch off about enough to make a biscuit and "roll between your hands and then flatten it out until it is about ½ inch thick." Place biscuits in flat pan or cookie sheet. Place pan (or cookie sheet) under broiler and *brown fast*. Put pan up in top oven and bake for 15 minutes.

Herman would rather eat 'Cile's corn bread than anything in the world.

Mama's Brunswick Stew

As there are usually 50 people at least at our pig-pickin' parties, Mama's recipe is here multiplied several times. This is what we cook on the kitchen stove for the crowd, keeping it hot in the old iron washpot over a wood fire. The guests have fun serving themselves from the pot with a long-handled soup dipper.

3 hens, 5 pounds each	2 tablespoons sugar
1 hog's head	2 tablespoons Tabasco
1 large bottle ketchup	½ cup apple vinegar
4 pounds okra	3 tablespoons Worcestershire
2 gallons canned tomatoes	sauce
2 onions, grated	1 gallon white creamed-style
5 unpeeled lemons, cut in pieces	corn

Boil hens in water to cover; save broth. Bone hens and cut into serving pieces. Boil and bone hog's head. Drain. Discard *this* broth. Add all ingredients except corn (including the boned hens and hog's head) to the broth from the hens. Cook at least 3 hours on top of the stove over *very low heat*. This can be done the day before and reheated for the party in whatever pot you plan to use. Add the gallon of creamed corn 1 hour before serving.

Chitlins
(Known as "Chitterlings" in intellectual circles)

I once heard that Craig Claiborne, the New York Times food expert, said that he would like to find a good way to cook chitlins.

I accept the challenge. I'm not a great chitlins lover myself, but I do serve them occasionally. Just knowing that chitlins are the small intestines of a hog puts some people off when it comes to preparing or eating them.

It is best to cook chitlins a day ahead unless you have a good neighbor who has a well-ventilated kitchen and no sense of smell!

Here's the recipe for a 5-pound bucket of chitlins.

First, clean well and place them with an onion in a deep pot. Add just enough water (salted and peppered to taste) to cover. Simmer gently until tender, about 2 or 3 hours. Drain and serve.

Some people like to eat them plain. But I prefer:

Batter-Fried Chitlins

Drain cooked chitlins (above) on paper towels. Roll them in dry flour and drop them in hot fat and fry until they are golden brown. Drain them on paper towels. Place them in the oven to keep warm until ready to serve. Serve them with vinegar or hot sauce.

For Extra-Fancy Chitlins, see page 125.

Barbecued Ham or Shoulder

Start with fresh shoulders or hams. The shoulder is more succulent and cheaper, so we usually use it for big parties. It helps to have a good neighbor who will patiently watch over the long cooking process. This method can be used for 12- to 18-pound hams or shoulders or for a whole pig. For our pig-pickin' party we cook both hams and shoulders in this manner:

1. Dig a hole in the ground 6 inches deep, 24 inches wide and 4 feet long. Use kindling to build a fire, until you have enough coals to burn green oak or hickory wood. Place a grill (we use an old bedspring) over the pit, 24 inches above ground level.

2. Over a low fire place meat, skin side up, on grill; cook very slowly until meat is warm on top side. Meat should never be over 130° F. to 150° F. at the bone. Do not turn meat until it is warm throughout (approximately 12 hours).

3. Turn and brown skin. After 16 hours' cooking time, start basting meat with Country Barbecue Sauce (below). Continue to baste and brown, turning as needed. Total cooking time: approximately 18 to 20 hours.

Country Barbecue Sauce

1¼ cups ketchup	*2 tablespoons dry mustard*
⅔ cup salad oil	*3 teaspoons grated fresh ginger*
1 cup vinegar, cider or wine	*1 clove garlic, minced*
5 tablespoons Worcestershire sauce	*1 lemon, sliced thin*
	3 tablespoons butter
1 cup brown sugar	*salt and pepper to taste*

Put all ingredients into a pot and heat until blended and the flavors get married! Baste the fresh shoulder or ham with it during the last couple of hours before serving. Serve some hot on the side, too.

This sauce is also excellent for barbecued Grilled Pork Loin (p. 106), Spareribs (p. 113) and as a marinade for basting Southern Barbecued Chicken (p. 138).

'Cile's Candied Apples

*Hard as I try, I simply can't make candied apples like 'Cile.
She says this is all she does:*

Take 6 to 8 apples; peel, cut in half and remove center seed core.
Sprinkle bottom of a baking dish with 1 teaspoon cinnamon, 1 teaspoon lemon juice, 1 cup sugar. Dot with small bits of butter. Place
apple halves, cut side down, in the baking dish and sprinkle a little
more sugar and cinnamon on top. Bake at 350° F. for 30 to 35 minutes.

Crusty Sweet Potato Casserole

3 cups sweet potatoes	*1 teaspoon vanilla*
1 cup sugar	*½ cup milk*
½ teaspoon salt	*2 eggs*
⅓ stick margarine	

Peel, slice and cook sweet potatoes. Drain. Add sugar, salt, margarine,
vanilla, milk and eggs.

Mix in mixer or mash and whip by hand. Pour into casserole and
top with the following:

1 cup brown sugar	*⅓ stick margarine*
½ cup self-rising flour	*1 cup chopped nuts*

Mix all ingredients together. Spread over potato mixture. Bake in
300° F. oven for 30 to 35 minutes or until brown to make a crunchy
topping. Serves 6.

Grandmother Shingler's Liver Pudding

Take 1 hog liver, lights (lung) and 1 hog jowl. Boil all together until
tender. Remove meat from jowl. Cut by hand into small pieces, then
grind in food chopper. Add 1½ to 2 cups of cooked rice and 1 medium-
size onion, chopped fine. Salt and pepper to taste. Mix well. Pack into
a bowl or loaf pan and refrigerate.

Kitty Brewster's Pickles

Slice as thin as possible:

1 gallon cucumbers (14 or 15)   *8 small onions*

Chop fine:

2 green peppers

Place in crock or other container (stonewear or glass) in thin layers, sprinkling ½ cup salt throughout all layers:

1 layer ice   *1 layer onion*
1 layer cucumber   *1 layer green pepper*

Cover with lid and let rest for 3 hours. Drain.

Bring to boil:

  5 cups vinegar   *1½ teaspoons ground cloves*
  5 cups sugar   *1½ teaspoons mustard seed*
1½ teaspoons turmeric   *2 teaspoons celery seed*

Add cucumber mixture to syrup and bring back to a light boil. Remove from heat and pack in glass jars.

Miniature Pecan Tassies

CRUST

1 3-ounce package cream cheese   *1 stick butter or margarine*
1 cup sifted plain flour

Have all ingredients at room temperature. Mix together and chill for at least 2 hours. Pinch off dough and shape into 2 dozen 1-inch balls. Place balls in 1¾-inch ungreased muffin tins. With your thumb, press dough against bottom and sides of tins. Set aside and mix filling.

FILLING

  1 egg, beaten   *1 tablespoon soft butter*
¾ cup brown sugar, firmly   *1 tablespoon vanilla*
    packed   *⅔ cup chopped pecans*

Mix all ingredients together. Fill each tassie ¾ full. Bake at 325° F. for 25 minutes. Cool on cake rack. To remove, run sharp knife around edge and lift out. Yield: 24 miniature tassies.

3

Perle Mesta Gets Her Grits

WHEN PERLE MESTA REIGNED SUPREME, Washington parties were grand affairs. Tables were laden with the best dishes of French and American cuisines, along with fine wines and fancy desserts.

I introduced something different. Back in those days, few had ever even heard of Georgia country cooking, and fewer still had ever tasted it. Sometimes I would bring 'Cile up from the farm when we were having a big Washington party. She loved the trip and I could relax knowing everything would taste just as it does in Lovejoy and that it wouldn't be anything like the catered food so often served by Washington hostesses.

In the days before "health foods" became so popular, guests would first look at the baked grits and wonder what it was. Then they'd taste it and want the recipe. You couldn't buy grits in most stores "up North" then, so I'd always have a few bags on hand. Incidentally, bags of grits keep well in the freezer.

One time I planned a dinner for my friend from Florida, Flo Davis. I invited several Senators' wives, along with Senator Margaret Chase Smith and Perle Mesta. I gave them the full farm fare and Perle Mesta fell in love with the cheese grits. She wanted some to serve at home. So, as she left the party, I slipped her a package. Flo had her camera handy and snapped a picture, so we have a record of "the hostess with the mostess" going home carrying a bag of grits under her arm! Even though it wasn't anyone's birthday, I served the Talmadge birthday dessert specialty that night.

Perle leaves my party with a bag of grits.

The pig and I at Dee Dot Ranch.

BACK-TO-THE-FARM DINNER
UP IN WASHINGTON

Southern Fried Chicken
Fresh Corn Casserole
Fresh Tomatoes and Cucumbers on Lettuce
Sweet Potato Biscuits
Baked Cheese Grits (p. 27)
Talmadge Peach Ice Cream
molded into the shape of a cake

Southern Fried Chicken

Soak chicken parts in salt water to cover in refrigerator overnight, if possible, or for at least 2 hours. Drain. Roll pieces in flour. Sprinkle with pepper.

Heat lard to smoking point in a heavy skillet or fryer. It should be at a depth of 2 inches in the pan. Drop in chicken pieces quickly. Cover. Fry for 15 minutes, or until you hear a noise like water being poured in it—that is the signal to turn chicken. Turn and brown other side about 15 minutes. Keep the heat high and cook it fast. As far as I am concerned, this is the only way to fry chicken.

45

Fresh Corn Casserole

6 *slices bacon*
8 *ears fresh corn, cut from cob,*
   and cob scraped for juices
¾ *cup chopped green pepper*
½ *cup chopped onion*

1 *teaspoon salt*
½ *teaspoon pepper*
2 *firm, ripe tomatoes, peeled and*
   sliced

In a large skillet, cook bacon until browned. Remove from skillet, drain on paper towels and crumble. Remove all but 2 tablespoons bacon fat from skillet. Add corn, green pepper and onion. Cook over high heat for 5 minutes. Add crumbled bacon, salt and pepper. In a 2-quart casserole, alternate layers of the corn mixture and the tomato slices. Bake uncovered in 350° oven 30 to 40 minutes, until all flavors are well blended. Serves 6.

Sweet Potato Biscuits

¼ *cup cool melted butter*
¾ *cup mashed cold sweet*
   potatoes
⅔ *cup milk*
1¼ *cup all-purpose flour*

2½ *teaspoons double-acting*
   baking powder
1 *tablespoon sugar*
1 *teaspoon salt*
¼ *teaspoon grated orange rind*

Preheat oven to 450° F. Beat butter into sweet potatoes. Stir in the milk. Sift flour with baking powder, sugar and salt. Stir in grated orange rind. Add sifted ingredients and rind to sweet potato mixture to form a dough. Turn dough on floured board and toss lightly; pat or roll to ¼-inch thickness. Cut into biscuits with biscuit cutter. Brush tops with melted butter before baking. Bake for 15 minutes.

Sweet potato biscuits will not be high and fluffy as the sweet potatoes are too heavy to let the dough rise very much. Yield: 16 to 18 biscuits.

Talmadge Peach Ice Cream

2 cups sugar
2 tablespoons flour
2 cups milk
4 eggs

2 large cans evaporated milk
*12 overripe peaches, peeled and
    mashed*
whipped cream or Cool Whip

Mix sugar and flour; add the milk and cook in double boiler until mixture steams.

Beat eggs; gradually add some of the hot mixture to them until the eggs are heated; pour back into double boiler. Cook until mixture coats spoon, stirring constantly.

Remove from heat and add the 2 cans of evaporated milk; pour into freezer container.

When mixture is frozen to a thick consistency, add peaches, which have been peeled and mashed thoroughly. The peaches should be *crushed*—and the riper the better, short of the fermentation stage. It may be necessary to add sugar to peaches, depending on individual taste.

Press into an angel-food pan or other mold to form birthday "cake" and freeze. Just before serving, decorate with a layer of whipped cream or Cool Whip. Slice like a cake.

Note: This ice cream is best made in a hand or electric freezer. If you do not have a freezer, however, put mixture in a deep ice tray in the freezing compartment of your refrigerator. When it becomes mushy, spoon into a bowl and beat with egg beater. Freeze and beat again. Then put in mold for final freezing.

PRESIDENTIAL PIG

Governor Christopher S. Bond of Missouri sent President Ford a country-cured ham with this message:
"I've often said that becoming a Missouri ham is the best thing that can happen to a pig."

4

Senate Wives' Luncheons on Capitol Hill

THE WATERGATE HEARINGS might have placed a strain on the wives involved, but women in Washington weather too many political storms to part over issues. Friendship among Senate wives is strictly bipartisan.

One of the reasons we have strong ties is the Senate wives' unit of the Red Cross. The wife of the Vice-President is always head of the group. We get together weekly to hand-roll bandages and make baby clothes for the Red Cross. We meet in one of the rooms on the first floor of the old Senate Office Building and work through lunch. Most of us bring a brown-paper-bag lunch from home, but once in a while we have a real party.

I decided, in the middle of the Watergate hearings, that Pat Nixon was going through a rough time and that she might like to relax with some of her old friends for lunch. The ones I invited, along with Mrs. Mamie Eisenhower, had been particularly close to Pat when she was the Vice-President's wife and in charge of our Red Cross unit. I had a table for eight in the middle of the Senate Dining Room reserved for us. We talked about the "early years," our children and/or grandchildren, and no one mentioned a word about the hearings that were going on.

The Senate Dining Room prepared most of the luncheon, but I did bring along some homegrown tomatoes from the farm and a batch of creole pralines made from a recipe Senator Allen Ellender (D., La.) gave me. He was President pro tem of the Senate then, but I think he liked his reputation as a superchef the best.

So many Senators and friends came over from other tables to

Friendship among Senate wives is bipartisan at this luncheon for First Lady Pat Nixon.

greet Mrs. Nixon that she hardly had time to eat a bite. We were told it was the first time in history that a First Lady had been entertained in the Senate Dining room while her husband was President.

SENATE DINING ROOM LUNCHEON

Stuffed Fillet of Sole
Corn Bread Muffins
Homegrown Tomatoes
Cold Asparagus Salad
Fresh Strawberries Laced with Bourbon (p. 29)
Senator Ellender's Creole Pralines

Stuffed Fillet of Sole

1 pound shrimp, sliced fine
1 pound crabmeat, picked over
to remove bone, cartilage
½ cup celery, diced

½ cup mayonnaise
salt and pepper to taste
6 pounds fillet of sole, sliced
thin

Combine shrimp, crabmeat, celery and mayonnaise to make a stuffing. Season. Spoon stuffing onto thin slice of fillet of sole and top with another fillet, until all are used. Place in well-buttered baking dishes. Dot with bits of butter. Bake for 15 minutes in 325° F. oven. Top with Blender Hollandaise Sauce (p. 26) and brown briefly under broiler. Serves 18.

ANTONIO COIA
Senate Dining Room Chef

Corn Bread Muffins

¾ cup sifted flour
2½ teaspoons baking powder
1 tablespoon sugar
½ teaspoon salt

1¼ cups cornmeal
1 egg
2 tablespoons melted butter
1 cup buttermilk

Preheat oven to 425° F. Grease muffin tins with oil and place in oven.

Sift dry ingredients together. Add beaten egg and butter. Then add buttermilk. Mix together, pour into hot muffin tins and bake for 25 minutes. Makes 20 small muffins.

Cold Asparagus Salad

⅔ *cup white vinegar*
½ *cup sugar*
½ *teaspoon salt*
1 *teaspoon whole cloves*
½ *teaspoon ground cinnamon*
1 *tablespoon celery seed*

½ *cup water*
2 *large cans (1 pound 3 ounces each) asparagus or 3 pounds cooked fresh asparagus*
pimiento

Combine all ingredients in saucepan except asparagus and pimiento; heat to boiling. Drain asparagus and place in flat baking dish; pour boiling liquid over asparagus, cover and place in refrigerator overnight or for 24 hours.

Before serving, drain well and garnish with sliced pimiento. Serves 10.

Senator Ellender's Creole Pralines

2 *cups granulated sugar*
1 *cup dark- or light-brown sugar*
1 *stick (¼ pound) butter*
1 *cup milk*

2 *tablespoons light corn syrup*
4 *cups pecan halves (if large halves, break into smaller pieces)*

Put all ingredients except the pecans in a 3-quart saucepan and cook for about 20 minutes after boiling starts, stirring occasionally. Add the pecans and continue to cook the mixture until it forms a soft ball when a little is dropped into cold water. Stir well and then drop by spoonfuls on waxed paper. Place a few sheets of newspaper beneath the waxed paper. (I find it convenient to place a small table near the stove, over which I put a few sheets of newspaper, and then put the waxed paper over that.) When cool, remove from waxed paper.

SENATE WIVES' RED CROSS VOLUNTEERS LUNCHEON

Magnolia Ham
Southern Fried Chicken (p. 45)
Baked Cheese Grits (p. 27)
Cucumber Mousse
Pecan Tassies (p. 42)

PINNING A MAGNOLIA ON A YANKEE HAM

One highlight of my Senate wives' Red Cross unit days was the time Lady Bird Johnson, then wife of the Vice President, asked me to be Chairman of the luncheon honoring First Lady Jacqueline Kennedy. Another memorable occasion was when we gave a surprise luncheon for Judy Agnew who, as the Veep's wife, headed our group at that time. None of us knew—not even Judy—that her husband would announce his resignation the next day. (We learned later that he had in fact postponed his resignation so as not to spoil the party we were giving Judy!)

I was in charge of the menu and I suspected we would have more than our usual thirty guests, but I didn't expect seventy. I brought the ham—a large one of the canned variety that I was marketing through my new enterprise, Betty Talmadge & Associates. It didn't look "natural" like my country-cured hams, so I decided to add a Southern touch. Maryon Allen, wife of Alabama's Senator James Allen, suggested the following creation.

I fixed it up with a glaze of peach juice, brandy and plain gelatin and garnished it with chopped peanuts and brandied peach halves.

I call this "Pinning a Magnolia on a Yankee Ham." I believe in putting a little romance into food. The ham was delicious and

A picture I cherish with two great First Ladies.

disappeared fast. Because of the crowd, we had ham slivers instead of slices.

Some of the other members brought food, too. Maryon Allen brought Southern corn bread. Rea Childs, wife of Florida Senator Lawton Childs, came with fresh biscuits.

We depended on Tony Coia, Italian chef of the Senate Dining Room, to provide Southern fried chicken, a casserole of cheese grits, and cucumber mousse. We turned him into a country cook with our own recipes! He may even have a Southern accent by now.

Magnolia Ham

Here's the way I gave the ham a Southern accent for the Senate wives' luncheon.

½ *cup brandy*	*1 canned ham (8-pound size)*
1 can (30 ounces) freestone peaches	*2 packages plain gelatin*
	1 cup chopped peanuts

Pour ½ cup brandy into bowl with the peaches and the peach liquid. Let it stand overnight if possible.

Sprinkle two packages gelatin over cold water in a small saucepan. Place over low heat and stir until gelatin dissolves (about 3 minutes).

Remove from heat and add peach juice-and-brandy mixture, reserving drained peaches to decorate the top.

Remove ham from can. Pour half the gelatin-juice-brandy mixture back in the can from the ham and refrigerate. Allow it to set and then remove and place it on top of ham. Press chopped peanuts into gelatin. Arrange peach halves over and around the ham, pour remainder of gelatin-juice-brandy mixture over them, refrigerate and allow to set.

Cucumber Mousse

5 large cucumbers	*1 tablespoon sugar*
2 cups ginger ale	*1 cup sour cream*
2 packages lime gelatin	*1 cup mayonnaise*
2 packages plain gelatin	*tomatoes for garnish*
Tabasco sauce—heavy dash	

Peel and grate cucumbers and drain for 1 hour. Add half the ginger ale. Heat the remainder of the ginger ale, dissolve plain and lime gelatin in it and add to the cucumber-ginger ale mixture. Cool. Mix in all other ingredients. Pour into a large, fancy mold.

This mousse looks and tastes cool—a perfect summer salad. (The dash of Tabasco is the mystery ingredient.) Surround mousse with sliced tomatoes. Serves 12.

5

Good Luck Buffet for New Year's Day

I'M USUALLY BACK in Georgia over the Christmas and New Year holidays, but wherever I am, you can be sure that I will have black-eyed peas on New Year's Day for good luck during the coming year.

Gwen and Jim Bentley, long-time friends of mine, have often kept the pots simmering on their country-kitchen stove for any number of drop-ins on the day after the New Year's Eve celebrations. If they don't have the party, I do. Whether I have open house in Washington or Lovejoy, or whether the party is at the Bentleys' historic house (the oldest in Atlanta), the buffet for from twenty to fifty—we never know how many may come—is always the same.

Most of the preparation and cooking is done well in advance. We leave the simmering pots on the kitchen stove during all of New Year's Day. Family and friends who stop by from noon until late evening serve themselves. Most of them even return their plates to the kitchen and pop them in the dishwasher.

All recipes in this section are for a buffet for twenty to fifty New Year's Day drop-ins. So far we've never run out of food.

NEW YEAR'S DAY
GOOD LUCK BUFFET

"Pot Likker"
Roast Pork with Apple Brandy
Black-eyed Peas with Hog Jowl
Candied Tomato Sauce
Turnip Greens with Ham Bone
Rutabagas
Artichoke Relish
Pepper Sauce
Fresh Vegetable Relish Tray
Cracklin' Corn Bread Muffins
Ambrosia
White Fruit Cake

"Pot Likker"

Using a long-handled dipper, remove excess juices from cooked turnip greens (Turnip Greens with Ham Bone, p. 58) and put this liquid into a stewpot or copper saucepan. Skim off grease, if necessary. Taste for additional salt and pepper. Add 1 tablespoon lemon juice and 1 teaspoon Pepper Sauce (p. 59) per quart of broth. Place on back burner over low heat to keep warm. Serve by ladling into teacups with 1 thin slice of lemon in each cup. Sip, or use a soup spoon.

Roast Pork with Apple Brandy

Use a good fresh lean pork, such as a 12-pound shoulder, a fresh ham or a huge backbone. Sprinkle generously with salt and freshly ground black pepper. Place in roasting pan. Add to pan 1 cup apple brandy or wine and 1 cup of water, or 2 cups of apple juice. There should be at least ½ inch of liquid in the bottom of the pan. Cover with heavy-duty aluminum foil, seal around edges and roast in 450° oven for 20 minutes; then reduce heat to 250°. Continue to roast for 3 to 4 hours until *well done*. Remove foil. Turn oven up to 325° or 350°. Allow to roast, uncovered, for an additional ½ hour or more, basting occasionally with pan juices. Allow to rest for 10 minutes or so before slicing (this will be simplified if you have an electric knife). If gravy is desired, add apple juice, stock or water to drippings, after skimming grease from top. Thicken with 1 or 2 tablespoons flour if you wish.

Black-eyed Peas with Hog Jowl

Pick over and rinse 2 pounds black-eyed peas. Soak for 2 or 3 hours, or preferably overnight. Boil ½ pound hog jowl and ¼ pound country-cured ham hock or ham bone for at least 30 minutes to make a good broth. Add drained peas, 1 large, peeled Bermuda onion, salt and pepper. Bring to boil; reduce to a simmer and cook at least 1 hour. This dish is even better if cooked a day earlier, refrigerated overnight and reheated to serve. We sometimes leave the pot on the back porch on cold winter nights.

Candied Tomato Sauce

Place at least 1 quart canned whole tomatoes with their juice in a large skillet. Add 1 large can tomato sauce. Bring to boil. Add 1 stick butter or margarine, 1 cup brown sugar, 1 cup white sugar or honey, juice of 2 or 3 lemons, juice of 1 orange, salt and pepper. Bring to boil again, then reduce heat to medium or low to maintain a hard simmer. Cook for about 1 hour until reduced to a good sauce, stirring frequently to avoid sticking, especially during last ½ hour of cooking time.

Spoon sauce on cooked greens, turnips and pork dishes. It is even better if cooked a day or two ahead, refrigerated, then reheated to serve. Yield: 1¼ quarts.

Turnip Greens with Ham Bone

Pick over and thoroughly rinse 1 fully packed peck of turnip greens (or 3 parts turnip greens to 1 part mustard greens). Rinse several times, until water is clean and *not gritty*. In extra-large pot, boil ½ pound of country-cured ham hock and a slice of hog jowl to make a good broth, using plenty of water to take into account evaporation and, later, preparation of "pot likker." Add greens. Salt to taste. Add a rounded teaspoon of sugar. Cook for 2 or 2½ hours at a steady simmer. Drain broth for "pot likker," and chop greens with scissors or sharp knife. Serve with Pepper Sauce (p. 59).

Rutabagas

Peel, slice and rinse 1 large or 2 medium rutabagas, and 4 or 5 white garden turnips. Boil a slice of country-cured ham hock in a quart of water 30 to 40 minutes for a good broth. Add rutabagas and turnips, salt and pepper to taste, a pinch of sugar and 3 tablespoons lemon juice. Cook at a steady simmer for 1 to 1½ hours. Remove ham hock. Mash rutabaga and turnips with a potato masher. Add 3 to 4 tablespoons country butter and mash again. Serve with ham hock.

We usually cook this a day or so ahead, refrigerate, and reheat to serve. Great with Candied Tomato Sauce (p. 57). Serves about 25.

Artichoke Relish

Scrub and scrape clean 4 quarts Jerusalem artichoke roots. Grind or chop fine with 4 large onions and 3 stalks of celery. Mix 2 tablespoons celery salt, ½ teaspoon red pepper, 2½ cups brown sugar, 1 teaspoon turmeric, 4 tablespoons salt, 1 tablespoon allspice and 1½ pints vinegar. Add to artichokes.

Simmer about 30 minutes, or until liquid thickens. Refrigerate or pack in about 8 sterilized pint jars and process 10 minutes in simmering hot-water bath.

This is a magnificent relish mixed in with vegetable and bean soups, as well as vegetables; use also as a spread in sandwiches with meats.

Pepper Sauce

Make this with small whole fresh green hot peppers from summer garden or vegetable market. We use a hot, hot pepper grown from seeds brought from Spain by my neighbor in Lovejoy, Louise Hastings. Save containers such as ketchup bottles or large soy-sauce bottles. Fill sterilized bottles almost to the top with clean, fresh peppers. Pour to the top boiling hot liquid made from 1 part apple-cider vinegar, 1 part sherry or Madeira, ½ teaspoon olive oil and ½ teaspoon mustard seeds.

Seal bottles and "cure" for five or six days. Add more liquid during the year as sauce is used. We just add more sherry. Shake or sprinkle *very* lightly on cooked vegetables and in soups. No need to refrigerate.

Fresh Vegetable Relish Tray

We garnish our New Year's Day buffet dishes with fresh raw vegetables. Spring onions are a must; then we add bell pepper strips, radishes, yellow squash, cauliflower or whatever is available. With or without a dip, these are good—and they go well with peas, greens, turnips and pork.

Cracklin' Corn Bread Muffins

Mix together 3 cups self-rising yellow cornmeal, ½ cup flour, 1 pound finely chopped pork cracklin's, 2 tablespoons melted shortening, 2 beaten eggs, 1 teaspoon white sugar and enough milk (or buttermilk if available) to thin sufficiently and pour into greased muffin tins.

Bake in preheated oven, about 450° to 475°, until browned, approximately 15 minutes. Makes about 36 muffins.

Ambrosia

Peel 3 or 4 dozen large, heavy oranges. Use a good sharp knife to remove rind and all white skin. Separate the sections from membranes, remove seeds, and put sections in large punch bowl. Add any juice left from peeling into bowl. Now, add 2 or 3 8-ounce packages of frozen or canned grated coconut and 2 cups white sugar to orange sections (or sweeten to taste because the sweetness of oranges varies). Fresh ground coconut, if available, can be used instead of the frozen or canned. Refrigerate in gallon jars. We usually prepare 2 gallons at a time. It keeps very well for weeks.

White Fruit Cake

Cream together ½ pound butter and 1 cup sugar. Sift together 1¾ cups flour and ½ tablespoon baking powder, and add with 5 beaten eggs to creamed butter-and-sugar mixture. Add 1 tablespoon vanilla, 1 tablespoon orange flavoring, 1 pound crystallized cherries, 1 pound crystallized pineapple, 4 cups walnuts or pecans, and 1 cup white raisins. Mix well and pour into two well-greased loaf (9″ by 5″ by 3″) pans lined with greased waxed paper.

Bake at about 300° F. for ½ hour, reduce heat to 250° F. and continue to bake for about 2½ hours.

Remove from oven and immediately add at least 1 cup strong brandy, liquor or sherry per loaf pan while cake is still warm in pan. Cool, remove cake in waxed paper from pan and wrap tightly in aluminum foil. Store in refrigerator or cool place. We like to mellow this cake for at least 3 weeks. It will keep for months.

6

Soups, Snacks and Salads

SOUPS

Senate Restaurant Famous Bean
    Soup
Peanut Soups (Plain, Fancy and
    Plantation)

Tomato Soup
Watercress Soup

SNACKS

Cheese Balls
Cheese Dates
Cheese Puffs
Chicken Liver Pâté
Ham Puffs with Peanut Butter
Ham with Melon Balls

Hot Pennies
Rosalynn Carter's "Plains
    Special" Cheese Ring
1-2-3 Sausage Balls
Sausage Pinwheels
Sesame Cheese Straws

SALADS

Cranberry Christmas Wreath
Salad Beets
Molded Beet Salad
Jellied Cabbage and Carrot Salad
Golden Apricot Molds
Orange Peanut Slaw
Pear Salad
Perfection Salad
Pork Salad

Spinach Salads
    Basic Dressing and Poppy Seed
        Dressing
Sliced Salad
    Marinade
Vegetable Salad Ring
Waldorf Salad
Wilted Lettuce

SOUPS

WHEN I'M HAVING a small luncheon, I usually serve soup—Watercress Soup or Peanut Soup are favorites—along with a cheese snack. Some quick and easy recipes are in the section that follows.

The Senate Dining Room was my mainstay when visitors came to Washington. We usually let them sightsee on their own and then meet for lunch at the Capitol. The food is good and the company around us—Senators and other dignitaries, along with lobbyists and home folks who are visiting—make any day in the dining room an event for an out-of-towner.

I always encourage our guests to start with the Famous Senate Bean Soup. It's a law that it must be on the Senate Dining Room menu everyday. Just for the asking, you can get a card with the recipe now when you eat there. It looks like this:

The Famous Senate Restaurant Bean Soup Recipe

Take two pounds of small Michigan Navy Beans, wash, and run through hot water until Beans are white again. Put on the fire with four quarts of hot water. Then take one and one-half pounds of Smoked Ham Hocks, boil slowly approximately three hours in covered pot. Braise one onion chopped in a little butter, and, when light brown, put in Bean Soup. Season with salt and pepper, then serve. Do not add salt until ready to serve. (Eight persons.)

Peanut Soup Plain

1½ *cups peanut butter*
1 *quart milk*
½ *teaspoon salt*

freshly ground pepper
½ *teaspoon vegetable seasoning*
   mixture

In pan over low heat, soften peanut butter to allow easy mixing with milk. Add milk, salt, pepper and vegetable seasoning mixture. Chill. Serves 8.

Peanut Soup Fancy

1 onion, chopped
2 celery stalks, chopped
3 tablespoons butter
3 tablespoons flour

1 quart chicken broth (or fresh chicken stock)
½ cup peanuts, chopped

Sauté onion and celery in butter; stir in flour. Add chicken stock, stirring constantly, until it comes to a boil. Remove from heat and combine with ingredients in Peanut Soup Plain (above). Return to low heat and cook till all ingredients are well blended. Garnish with peanuts and serve hot or cold. Serves 12.

Plantation Peanut Soup

1 quart chopped celery
1 quart chopped onions
½ pound butter or margarine
1 cup all-purpose flour
1 gallon + 1 cup chicken broth
1 quart milk

1 quart light cream
1 quart peanut butter
½ teaspoon each salt, pepper, paprika
½ teaspoon Tabasco sauce

Simmer celery and onions slowly in butter or margarine in a large soup kettle. Make a paste of flour and the 1 cup of broth. Stir into celery and onions. Stir in remaining broth. Cook while stirring until mixture bubbles and thickens. Add milk, cream and peanut butter. Whip until smooth and creamy. Simmer (but do not boil) for about 5 minutes. Stir in salt, pepper and paprika. Finish off with ½ teaspoon Tabasco sauce. Serves 25.

Fresh Tomato Soup

This is easiest if you have a blender to puree the tomatoes, but you can do it using your electric beater or even by hand through a sieve or food mill.

Basic Cream Sauce
1 teaspoon salt
4 ripe tomatoes, peeled and diced
2 tablespoons chopped onion

1 teaspoon sugar
salt and pepper to taste
3 sprigs parsley

Make Basic Cream Sauce (p. 26), doubling the recipe and adding the 1 teaspoon salt. Puree tomatoes and onion and add to hot sauce, stirring constantly. Add sugar, salt and pepper to taste. Serve hot, topped with sprigs of parsley. Serves 4.

Watercress Soup

1 large bunch watercress (with stems removed and leaves chopped)
2 tablespoons chopped green onions

2 14-ounce cans chicken broth
¼ teaspoon salt
½ teaspoon sugar
1 cup milk

If you have a blender, chopping the watercress and onions in it will be easier than doing this by hand. In that case, add ½ cup chicken broth to blender while chopping. Combine with remaining chicken broth (or all the broth at once, if you are making by hand), also adding the salt, sugar and milk. Simmer in a saucepan for 15 minutes to blend flavors. Serve hot or chilled. Serves 4 to 6.

SNACKS

Cheese Balls

1 pound soft Cheddar cheese
1 pound cream cheese
¼ pound blue cheese
¼ pound smoked cheese (any
cheese with smoked flavor
will do)

1 tablespoon prepared mustard
1 tablespoon onion salt
¼ teaspoon garlic salt
1 tablespoon horseradish
port wine to moisten
chopped nuts or parsley

Mix and mash together all ingredients except nuts or parsley and shape into small balls. Roll balls in nuts or parsley. Yield: approximately 30 balls.

Cheese Dates

When Lady Bird Johnson visited Virginia Callaway and the lovely Callaway Gardens in Pine Mountain, Georgia, these dates were served and Mrs. Johnson requested the recipe.

Cut 1 pound pitted dates in half and heat in well-greased saucepan until good and gooey. (Don't use prechopped dates—too much sugar.) Allow to cool while making this dough:

½ pound sharp cheese, grated
½ pound butter or margarine
1 teaspoon salt

½ teaspoon cayenne pepper
½ teaspoon paprika
2½ cups plain flour

Cream cheese and butter together. Add salt, pepper, paprika and flour. Roll thin. Roll ½ teaspoon date mixture at a time into ball or small stick and enclose in dough, being sure to seal edges well. Bake 15 to 20 minutes in 400° F. oven. Do not brown. These freeze well. Makes 60.

Cheese Puffs

½ *pound sharp cheese*　　　　¼ *teaspoon cayenne pepper*
¼ *pound margarine (softened)*　½ *teaspoon salt*
1¼ *cup (scant) flour*

Grate cheese, work margarine and cheese together using hands, then work in flour, cayenne and salt. Form into small balls. Bake at 350° F. for 15 minutes. This dough will keep indefinitely in refrigerator before baking, or it can be frozen. Makes 3½ dozen.

Chicken Liver Pâté

½ *pound chicken livers*　　　*salt*
2 *hard-boiled eggs*　　　　*freshly ground pepper*
3 *tablespoons sour cream or*　1 *small onion, chopped (optional)*
　mayonnaise

Simmer livers in water to cover until just done. Drain. Blend all ingredients together at medium speed until smooth. Pack into a small dish or mold. Chill before serving. Unmold if you wish.

Ham Puffs with Peanut Butter

1 *egg yolk*　　　　　　　¼ *teaspoon salt*
½ *cup ground ham*　　　　1 *egg white, stiffly beaten*
½ *cup peanut butter*　　　30 *round crackers*
1 *teaspoon grated onion*

Beat egg yolk well and mix with ham, peanut butter, onion and salt. Fold into beaten egg white. Put small spoonfuls on crackers and place on baking sheet. Bake at 350° F. for 10 minutes. Serve hot. Makes 30 puffs.

Ham with Melon Balls

6 to 8 ounces Talmadge country-
cured ham, cooked and thinly
shaved

1 large cantaloupe or medium
honeydew

Shave ham into strips about 4 by 1 inches. Cut melon into balls about
1 inch in diameter. Place on paper toweling to absorb moisture. Wrap
each ball with a strip of ham; secure with toothpicks. Chill and serve.
Makes 2 to 3 dozen balls.

Hot Pennies

1 stick (¼ pound) butter
½ pound sharp Cheddar cheese,
grated

½ envelope onion soup mix
1 cup flour
½ teaspoon salt

Let butter and cheese reach room temperature. Mix well. Add soup
mix, flour and salt. Mix again. Form into 1-inch-thick rolls. Chill. Slice
into ¼-inch rounds. Bake at 375° F. on ungreased baking sheet 10 to
12 minutes, or until slightly brown. Can be baked in advance and
warmed at serving time. Yield: 2 dozen.

Rosalynn Carter's "Plains Special" Cheese Ring

*I usually double this recipe to make a generous ring—or
sometimes use the single recipe to make a cheese log.*

1 pound sharp Cheddar cheese,
grated
1 cup chopped pecans or walnuts
1 cup mayonnaise

1 small onion, grated
black pepper to taste
dash of cayenne

Mix all ingredients together. Mold with hands into desired shape. A
ring is attractive and center can be filled. Place in refrigerator until

chilled. When ready to serve, fill center with strawberry preserves. Good also as a cheese spread without preserves.

1-2-3 Sausage Balls

1 pound hot sausage
2 cups finely grated sharp
   Cheddar cheese

3 cups prepared biscuit mix

Mix all ingredients well; I use my hands. Pinch off enough at a time to make 1-inch balls. Bake in preheated 425° F. oven for 10 to 12 minutes. You can also roll out this dough, cut it into small biscuits and bake. It's the same good taste either way. If you don't plan to serve these immediately, bake first, then freeze and reheat as needed. Yield: 30 balls.

Sausage Pinwheels

2½ cups biscuit mix
  ⅔ cup water

1 pound hot sausage

Make dough with biscuit mix and water. Roll into oblong 7 by 12 inches approximately ½ inch thick. Spread raw sausage across center of dough and roll into long "jelly roll." With scissors, cut rounds from roll ½ inch thick and place on cookie sheet. Bake in preheated 425° F. oven for 10 to 12 minutes. These may be frozen after baking and reheated when ready to serve. Yield: 2 dozen.

Sesame Cheese Straws

  1 cup sifted flour
½ teaspoon salt
¼ teaspoon dry mustard
⅛ teaspoon cayenne pepper

⅓ cup butter
  1 cup grated Cheddar cheese
1½ tablespoons water
  1 teaspoon sesame seeds

Preheat the oven to 350°. Sift flour, salt, mustard and cayenne into a bowl. Add butter and ½ cup of the cheese. Cut mixture to a coarse consistency. Add water. Toss mixture to shape into a ball. Roll to ⅛-inch thickness. Sprinkle with ¼ cup of the cheese. Fold over. Sprinkle with remaining cheese and fold over again. Roll to ⅛ inch thickness. Cut into 4 × ½-inch strips. Sprinkle with sesame seeds. Bake cheese straws on a cookie sheet 12 to 15 minutes. Yield: 5 to 6 dozen.

SALADS

Cranberry Christmas Wreath

I usually serve this colorful molded salad on spinach leaves with whole mint-flavored green-tinted pears in the middle for a holiday buffet.

1 pound fresh cranberries	*1 pound chutney, chopped*
2 cups sugar	*2 cups celery, chopped*
4 cups water	*2 cans (11 ounces each) mandarin*
3 envelopes unflavored gelatin	*oranges, drained*

Combine cranberries, sugar, and 2 cups water; simmer 10 minutes. Mix gelatin with remaining 2 cups water. Stir gelatin mixture into hot cranberries. Chill until slightly thickened. Add chutney, celery and oranges. Pour into a 2-quart ring mold and chill until firm. To unmold, dip mold into lukewarm water for a second or two and invert onto platter. Fill with pears as suggested above, or as desired. Serves 16.

Salad Beets

1 bunch beets (at least 1 pound)	*½ cup sugar*
1 pint white vinegar	

Boil beets until just tender. Peel, slice. Dissolve sugar in vinegar. Pour over beets. Refrigerate overnight. Use in salads or as desired.

Molded Beet Salad

This is a favorite with Herman's sister, Margaret Talmadge Shepherd, who finds it an easy one to prepare ahead.

1 #2 can beets, chopped (save juice)
2 tablespoons white vinegar
1 family-size package lemon-flavored gelatin
½ cup finely chopped celery
1 small onion, chopped fine
¼ cup finely chopped green pepper
½ cup grated carrots
salt

Measure beet liquid; add vinegar and water as necessary to make 1¾ cups. Bring to boil, remove from heat and dissolve lemon gelatin in it. Cool to partly thicken and add vegetables and salt. Pour into mold. Chill until firm. Unmold. Serve with a dressing made with equal parts mayonnaise and sour cream, adding horseradish to taste, if desired.

Jellied Cabbage and Carrot Salad

1 package lime-flavored gelatin
2 cups water, heated to boiling
⅓ cup white vinegar
1 tablespoon sugar
salt
freshly ground pepper
½ medium-size head cabbage, grated fine
3 carrots, grated fine
2 tablespoons mayonnaise

Dissolve gelatin in hot water; add vinegar, sugar, salt and pepper. Mix well. Stir in cabbage and carrots. Cool. Stir in mayonnaise. Pour into mold and refrigerate. Serves 8.

Golden Apricot Molds

3½ cups peeled apricot halves (1 # 2½ can)
¼ cup white vinegar
1 teaspoon whole cloves
4 inches stick cinnamon
1 package orange-flavored gelatin

Drain apricots, reserving syrup. Add vinegar and spices to syrup and bring to boiling. Add apricots and simmer 10 minutes. Remove apricots and place in 6 to 8 individual molds. Strain syrup mixture and measure; add enough hot water to make 2 cups. Pour over gelatin and stir until dissolved. Pour gelatin mixture over apricots; chill until firm. Turn out on slices of canned jellied cranberry sauce on lettuce. Serve with mayonnaise. Serves 6 to 8.

Orange Peanut Slaw

3 to 4 small oranges	*1 tablespoon sugar*
1 small head cabbage, shredded	*¾ cup mayonnaise*
½ cup salted peanuts	*½ teaspoon salt*
1 tablespoon lemon juice	

Peel oranges and cut into small pieces. Shred cabbage. Combine cabbage, orange pieces and peanuts. Mix remaining ingredients. Pour over slaw and mix lightly. Cover and refrigerate 20 to 30 minutes before serving. Serves 12.

Suggestion 1: The membrane on oranges comes off quickly and thoroughly if you drop whole peeled orange in boiling water for 1 or 2 minutes.

Suggestion 2: If you wish to use your blender for shredding, place quarters of cabbage in blender with water to cover; press "Shred" button. Remove from blender and drain off liquid. Takes only a minute and is very easy.

Pear Salad

Drain canned pears in quantity desired. Save juice for another use. Fill halves with cream cheese to which chopped pecans and preserved ginger have been added. Press halves together. Use a whole clove for the stem and a sprig of mint for the leaf. Serve on a bed of lettuce with mayonnaise.

Perfection Salad

2 *envelopes gelatin, dissolved in*
    ½ cup cold water
2 *cups water heated to boiling*
½ *cup vinegar*
2 *tablespoons lemon juice*
½ *cup sugar*

1 *teaspoon salt*
1 *cup shredded cabbage*
2 *cups celery*
2 *pimientos, chopped fine*
    olives, carrots, chopped nuts
    (optional)

Add hot water to dissolved gelatin. Combine with the rest of the ingredients. Pour into mold and refrigerate. Serves 8.

Pork Salad

3 *cups cooked and chopped pork*
    shoulder
½ *cup chopped celery*
⅓ *cup mayonnaise*
2 *tablespoons pickle relish*
1 *teaspoon prepared mustard*

⅓ *cup finely chopped onion*
1 *teaspoon Worcestershire sauce*
    salt to taste
    lettuce
¼ *cup pimiento or green pepper*

Mix pork and celery. Chill thoroughly. Mix in mayonnaise, relish, mustard, onion, Worcestershire, salt. Serve on lettuce. Garnish with pimiento or green pepper. Serves 6.

Spinach Salad #1

Fresh spinach leaves, washed and crisp from the refrigerator, make a salad-vegetable dish that completes any luncheon or dinner. The Basic Dressing, below, has a touch of dry mustard, and the spinach and the delicate flavor of mustard in the dressing go especially well with ham dishes.

2 *pounds fresh spinach, washed*
    and drained
4 *hard-boiled eggs, chopped*

8 *strips bacon, crisply fried and*
    crumbled

BASIC DRESSING

1 cup salad oil	*2 teaspoons chopped parsley*
5 tablespoons vinegar	*(optional)*
1½ teaspoons salt	*2 cloves garlic, crushed, or 2*
½ teaspoon dry mustard	*tablespoons grated onion*
½ cup sugar	*coarsely ground black pepper*

Mix all ingredients for dressing thoroughly. Refrigerate. This should be prepared at least 6 hours before using. Just before serving, toss spinach with desired amount of dressing. Top with chopped eggs and crumbled bacon. Serves 10 to 12.

Spinach Salad #2

2 pounds fresh spinach, washed	*1 ripe avocado, sliced*
and drained	*1 grapefruit, sectioned*

Combine spinach with avocado slices and grapefruit sections. Toss with Poppy Seed Dressing just before serving. Serves 10 to 12.

POPPY SEED DRESSING

Add 2 tablespoons poppy seeds to Basic Dressing, above, and refrigerate.

Spinach Salad #3

2 pounds fresh spinach, washed	*1 large onion, sliced in thin rings*
and drained	*4 hard-boiled eggs, chopped*
2 cups sliced water chestnuts	*½ pound bacon, fried crisp and*
1 cup bean sprouts (if canned,	*crumbled*
drain well)	

Combine all ingredients except bacon in a large bowl. Toss with dressing below and sprinkle bacon over the top. Serves 10 to 12.

(see next page for dressing)

DRESSING

1 cup salad oil	2 teaspoons salt
½ cup vinegar	⅓ cup ketchup
¾ cup sugar	

Combine all ingredients in a blender or whip in a bowl. Pour over Spinach Salad #3 in quantity desired and toss well.

Sliced Salad

6 medium-size white potatoes, boiled	6 tomatoes
	2 bell peppers, or 2 cucumbers
6 hard-boiled eggs	2 onions

Slice all ingredients. Alternate layers in salad bowl. Add Marinade, below, and marinate for 3 hours or more in the refrigerator. Serves 6 to 8.

MARINADE

½ cup oil	2 teaspoons paprika
½ cup white vinegar	salt and pepper to taste

Mix well and add to Sliced Salad as directed above.

Vegetable Salad Ring

1 pint boiling water	2 or 3 hard-boiled eggs, sliced
1 teaspoon salt	6 stuffed olives, sliced in rings
2 tablespoons white vinegar	½ cup grated raw carrot
1 package lemon-flavored gelatin	¼ cup sliced green onions
½ cup chopped green pepper or pimiento	½ cup chopped celery
	1 cup chopped cucumber

Add water, salt and vinegar to gelatin. When dissolved, pour about ½ of mixture into ring mold and allow to set in cool place. When firm, arrange over it the pepper or pimiento, the hard-boiled egg slices and the olives in an attractive design. Add just enough of remainder of gelatin mixture to cover, but not to float, the design, and again allow to set. Mix all other ingredients with remainder of gelatin and add to mold. Chill until firm. Unmold and serve on a bed of lettuce, filling center of ring with additional fresh vegetables if desired. Serves 6.

Waldorf Salad

1 cup mayonnaise
1 tablespoon sugar
1 teaspoon grated orange rind
½ teaspoon salt

½ cup chopped pecans
3 cups diced, unpeeled apples
2 cups shredded Cheddar cheese
½ cup diced celery

Cream mayonnaise, sugar, orange rind and salt. Add pecans, apples, cheese and celery and mix well. Chill. Serve over lettuce leaves. Serves 8.

Wilted Lettuce

4 or 5 slices bacon
¼ cup white vinegar
1 teaspoon chopped onion
2 tablespoons sweet or sour
  cream (optional)

lettuce leaves, washed, dried well
  and torn into serving-size pieces

Fry bacon until crisp. Remove from pan, drain, crumble and set aside. Leave drippings in pan. Add to drippings the vinegar, onion and cream, if used. Heat all gently, pour over lettuce leaves, adding the crumbled bacon. Toss together and serve at once.

VIRGINIA PORK FESTIVAL

The selection of the Virginia Pork Festival's Queen and Princess is more than just a beauty contest. Only girls whose parents are actively engaged in pork production can compete. Virginia farmers produce over 700,000 hogs annually for market purposes, mostly in southeastern Virginia in the peanut-corn belt.

PART II

Pigs Are My Business— From Curing to Cooking

ONE OF THE REWARDS of a pig slaughtering in southern Georgia when I was a child was the ball made from the pig's bladder. The folks would wash the bladder and, using a hollow straw (probably of oat or wheat), would blow the bladder up to about the size of a football. The fresh bladder would stretch. Then they would remove the straw, tie off the neck and hang the balloon up in a tree to dry. After a few days, the bladder would be as light as a feather and have the feel of parchment. Sometimes we children would insert some dried beans or peas before it was blown up and they would rattle inside. It didn't have too much bounce but we had a great time playing toss and catch with it!

Even though I must have witnessed pigs being slaughtered many times as a child, I wasn't prepared for my first adult experience in 1946. We had moved to the farm, and soon after we were settled, Herman presented me with three hogs. I was obviously destined to be a model farm wife. Just before he conveniently departed on a business trip, he suggested that it was time to slaughter the hogs and cure the hams.

The "ham house" was my home in the early days.

I called our farmhands together and we discussed the procedure. There were seven of us, and we had seven different ideas about how those hogs ought to be cut up and what should be done with them.

We struggled for hours, cutting the hams, grinding and seasoning the sausage and rendering the fat. Finally we finished at 3 A.M. I felt like a piece of lard!

It was a bit later that I entered the ham business seriously. But that experience helped me find the courage to do it. And when I did, I devised the best seasoning for sausage and the finest method of curing hams before we put them on the market. I'm a taste-tester, which is probably why I'm also a weight watcher! Perfection comes from experimentation. The ham business helped me bring old family recipes into current use.

My days as a farm wife were fewer than either Herman or I expected. Herman's father, Eugene Talmadge, had been elected Governor of Georgia for a fourth term. He became seriously ill and died soon after we moved to Lovejoy. We found ourselves thrown into the middle of a political turmoil over who would succeed Father Talmadge. The fight became so bitter that the Legislature had to settle it, and the legislators elected Herman Governor. I was only twenty-four and far from confident I could handle the job of First Lady.

We moved into the old Governor's Mansion, which was located then in the middle of Atlanta. Before I had found the pots and pans, Herman called from the State House and said he had invited the members of the Legislature and their wives to come over for a buffet dinner!

"How many did you say?" I asked.

"About four hundred," he replied.

Our whole budget for a month was six hundred dollars and I could see it disappearing in one gala party! But I knew better than to protest.

"When did you say they were coming?" I gasped.

"Tomorrow night."

I can't remember the details, but I do remember calling every good friend I had and asking each one to bake a ham or a cake or make a salad—anything I could serve.

I even called the manager of the Piedmont Driving Club and

borrowed pots, pans and napkins and other necessary items. My friends and I had cooked all night. The next day we were pretty well organized. And then Herman came home with the news that the dinner had to be postponed a week. The hams and turkeys went into the refrigerators, and we put it all together again a week later!

By the time we left the Governor's Mansion six years later I was accustomed to serving any number of guests at any time. The last party, like the first, set a record which I'm sure has yet to be matched. Herman's second term as Governor was drawing to a close and he wanted to have an open house, on December 20, 1954, as a last gesture of hospitality. We invited everyone from Lovejoy and Henry County. And, I believe, everyone came—despite a rare snowfall and slippery roads. We had 2,500 guests. With the freezing temperatures, we had a time getting them to file through the mansion. According to the records, they consumed 150 pounds of fruit cake, 4,000 pieces of candy, 10,000 party sandwiches, uncounted bowls of nuts and untold gallons of coffee.

Parties like these were always a success because I had found a formula: friends will help in any crisis. For example, my talented neighbor Louise Hastings has frequently decorated my tables with beautiful flower arrangements. Other friends have molded hundreds of sausage patties or chopped a mountain of cabbage for cole slaw or baked cookies and Sally Lunn bread.

But I'm always in charge of the ham. And we have ham whenever we entertain.

Herman and I had just started the ham business when he became Governor. We were processing country hams and selling them to stores and restaurants. As his work in public office became more demanding, he asked me to take over the whole Talmadge ham business. I had a few stocks and bonds, which I sold and put into the business, and from that day forward, I took charge of the ham operation. When my money became involved, so did I!

With the money raised from selling stocks, we started curing about two hundred hams. I put my house helper, Hattie, and her daughter, 'Cile (you'll find a number of her cooking ideas in this book), along with two young local girls, a supervisor and his wife, to work rubbing the formula into the hams.

Our special formula includes salt, because it brings the moisture

Herman and Kate Smith on an early TV show.

out, sugar for flavor, a bit of pepper, small amounts of nitrites and nitrates, and lots of elbow grease!

Early that summer the hams went into Atlanta restaurants, where they were an immediate success. That was in 1951. By the end of the year we had sold 6,000 hams and decided to expand for a nationwide market. We borrowed money to build a ham house approved by the Department of Agriculture and we were soon selling 1,200 hams a week and going strong.

We never had enough money for advertising so our chances of being nationally known were slim. But we had one opportunity, and unfortunately Herman passed it by. That was the time he appeared on Kate Smith's television program. He was being interviewed about whether he might run for United States Senator against Walter George.

He was not ready at the time to announce, so he said, "Well, I don't know."

They asked him what he *thought* he was going to do.

He replied, "I don't even know what I'm going to have for

breakfast in the morning, much less what I'm going to do a year from now."

Then the reporter asked Herman, "Well, what do you *think* you're going to have for breakfast?"

And there he was on national television and he said, "Eggs."

I was ready to kill him, because he could have at least said *Talmadge Ham and eggs!*

The ham business survived and so did Herman's political future. He was elected to the Senate in 1956.

Even as our business grew, one of our biggest problems was being short of working capital. We were about to go broke making a profit!

So I went to the Trust Company of Georgia in Atlanta to borrow $100,000. I was bug-eyed that I could even ask to borrow that much money. But within two years I had the money paid back and was beginning to sleep soundly again.

After the business had been going along for a few years, Herman happened to see John Sibley, then Chairman of the Board of the Trust Company of Georgia.

Mr. Sibley said, "Herman, I'm so glad that the ham venture is a success!"

Herman wondered why the Chairman of the Board of a large bank would be so well informed about such a relatively small business. So he asked: "How do you know we are so successful?"

Mr. Sibley replied, "Well, you have quit calling it *Betty's* business, and started calling it *our* business!"

For a long time I was the only woman, at least in the Southeast, trading in the meat business. I understand there are others today. But this was really to my advantage as long as I was dealing with a man who knew what he was doing and was sure of himself. I had a lot of interesting encounters with males along the way.

One time I was having trouble with some hams being sent to me from a large company. The hams were not properly trimmed. So I decided to go out to the company and correct the problem.

The plant manager offered to see me, but I told him he wasn't the one I wanted to talk to.

"I want to see the man who trims and cuts my hams. He's the fellow I want to deal with. We can get the problem straightened out, but I don't think it needs to go through three people."

So we went down and met a young man named Weyman. I proceeded to show Weyman how I wanted the hams trimmed and cut, and he understood what I wanted from that time on.

As I was leaving, Weyman turned to the plant manager and I heard him say, "I thought you said she was an old woman." I could just hear him say, "That old woman doesn't know what she wants." But in those days I was in my early thirties, and I certainly thought I was young. The point is, I got my hams the way I wanted them. We built a mutual respect for each other.

I'll never forget another time several years later I received a shipment of poorly trimmed hams from Armour and Company. They wanted to keep me as a customer (by then the business was flourishing) so they sent someone down to take a look.

A well-dressed young man arrived on the scene at the time when I was performing a menial, but necessary, duty—rubbing hams.

He said he would like to see Mrs. Talmadge. I was up to my elbows in grease and salt, trying to get the curing process started.

I looked up and said, "I'm Mrs. Talmadge."

"You're Mrs. Talmadge?" he said, obviously surprised.

However, after I had shown him the kind of job his company had done, and then handed him a knife so that he could help me properly trim the hams—he *knew* I was Mrs. Talmadge.

I figured if I was working on his company's mistakes, he could work too.

I didn't know until later that the man was a top vice-president of Armour. He had come down to Georgia more out of curiosity to see a woman in the ham business than for anything else. He still tells the story and enjoys it as much as I do.

As time went on, I was able to expand the business. I began to add new products and seek new markets. I went into sausage, and from that to bacon. Then, we started slicing the country ham and putting it into packages that were less expensive, and easier to prepare.

I believe there are as many men as women who enjoy ham products and know how to cook them. Once there was a ham competition where I was the only woman—that was the time I crashed a country ham contest in the U.S. Senate Dining Room! The Washington *Post* of April 24, 1969, spread the story clear across a page with the headline UNINVITED MOUSSE WINS SENATE HAM-FEST. It was a great day and so well reported by Kevin Klose that I'll just include the whole story:

At the U.S. Senate's country ham contest yesterday, the competition dissolved when an uninvited housewife with a recipe for ham mousse upstaged three U.S. Senators before a crowd of hungry reporters.

The contest was called by Sen. Marlow W. Cook (R., Ky.) after he fell into gentlemanly disagreement with Sen. Harry F. Byrd, Jr. (D., Va.) over the relative merits of their states' country hams.

Cook invited Byrd and a fellow Southerner, Sen. Howard H. Baker (R., Tenn.), to enter representative hams in a contest to determine which tasted better. The winner would be chosen by Senate Dining Room maitre d' Robert Parker after he served the ham in the Senate Dining Room.

The warm-up was in the steamy Senate kitchen, where three hams, elegantly sliced and garnished, stood ready for the luncheon test. About 20 reporters and cameramen milled about, helping themselves to platters of sliced ham, awaiting rhetorical send-offs for the samples from the Senators.

Baker and Byrd arrived to find Betty Talmadge, wife of Sen. Herman E. Talmadge (D., Ga.), beaming from behind a Georgia ham garnished with sliced Georgia peaches.

Talmadge, accompanying his wife, expressed mild indignation at not having received an invitation. Turning to Byrd, whose family owns one of the world's largest apple orchards, Talmadge remarked, "Forgetting us for a ham contest is like having an apple contest and forgetting you, Harry."

"I wasn't invited, so I invited myself," explained smiling Mrs. Talmadge. She sported a solid gold ham pin, which her husband said she'd won "the last time she entered one of these."

"I like them all," said Byrd, trying some of each for the cameramen. Cook, the senatorial contest originator, arrived after a long delay. "He's afraid he'll lose," jibed Talmadge.

"Okay, everybody eat at once," yelled a photographer.

"I brought my hams here in a rented limousine," said Baker affably, like a chef whose souffle hadn't collapsed.

"Mmmmmm," said a photographer, munching a Baker-supplied ham and biscuit and pointing a greasy finger at some garnish on the Talmadge ham. "What're those?"

"Why that's ham mousse," said Mrs. Talmadge. "Go ahead and try some."

The photographer did, juggling his battered camera in the greasy hand while reaching daintily with the other for the small, rolled ham slice containing the mousse. . . .

"Outta the way," said the photographer, reaching for another rolled mousse. "How'd ya say ya made these, Mrs. Talmadge?"

I never did answer that reporter's question. After the *Post* declared me the winner, I just couldn't confess the truth and let the Senators and members of the press who were present know that I didn't make the ham mousse. In fact, I don't even know the recipe. Since I hadn't been invited, I was determined that my ham would outshine all others. So, after I cooked it, I took it to a French chef and had him decorate it for me!

The mousse notwithstanding, I have cooked and cured, prepared and invented, collected and discarded more ham recipes than probably any other cookbook compiler. The cooking of pork products is a craft—each effort may turn out a bit different from the one before but most are interesting and delicious.

Ham, pork and bacon recipes are not to be found in great numbers in most cookbooks. The methods and time specified are often at great variance. Even choosing a ham can be complicated, because of the variety of names used to describe it. Fortunately, the U.S. Department of Agriculture has put out a list that clearly defines the various types of ham that can be found in an average market. I am including the definitions at the end of the book in the section "Facts, Charts, Metric Measures and other Miscellanea."

There are probably more misconceptions about pork than about any other meat. To begin with, hogs are bred leaner today than they were decades ago. The pork industry has had a hard time dispelling some of our grandmother's instructions to cook pork "a long time, at a high temperature," with the added warning: "Don't eat too much because it's fattening."

Not so! Pork cookery has changed. Today pork is cooked at low to moderate temperatures—the internal temperature for all fresh pork cuts to be roasted is 170° F., rather than the older 185° F. Research studies show that roasts cooked at the lower temperature are done in less time and are juicier. There is less shrinkage and cooking loss and, best of all, less spattering, which keeps the range cleaner.

And hogs are put on a stricter diet than most of us would like to consider for ourselves these days! Because of the feed programs utilizing scientific information on nutrient requirements, pork meats are leaner and have more nutritional value. In addition, pork is now recognized as having less saturated fat than many red meats and is highly digestible.

Because they mature earlier, pigs now develop less fat than did their predecessors. Most meat processors and retailers do a good job of trimming any excess fat long before it reaches you. Nutritionally, the meat that you purchase is an excellent source of all the B vitamins—thiamin (B_1), riboflavin (B_2), and $B6$ and $B12$. It is the richest known food source of thiamin. A high-quality protein, pork is also rich in iron, the mineral that plays a vital role in formation and maintenance of red blood cells and the prevention of anemia.

Nutritionists are now including various cuts of pork, right along with beef, veal and lamb, as meat for dieters—a $3\frac{1}{2}$-ounce pork loin chop contains only 250 calories. A 3-ounce serving of cured ham, fat trimmed off, contains about 160 calories.*

* "New Pork Calories Fewer," *The Atlanta Constitution,* March 11, 1976, p. 11-F; "Pork Has Place on Diet," *The Atlanta Constitution,* March 25, 1976, p. 21-F; "How Pork Cookery Has Changed," PIG Pork Industry Group, National Live Stock & Meat Board, 36 S. Wabash Avenue, Chicago, Ill., from a release dated August 1975.

THE BOAR'S HEAD

"The boar's head, in ancient times, formed the most important dish on the table, and was invariably the first placed on the board upon Christmas-day, being preceded by a body of servitors, a flourish of trumpets, and other marks of distinction and reverence, and carried into the hall by the individual of next rank to the lord of the feast."

—from Mrs. Isabella Beeton's Book of Household Management, *1861.*

1

Talmadge Country-Cured Ham

THERE ARE NO TWO PEOPLE who cook country-cured ham the same way. There are no two hams that will come out looking and tasting exactly the same, no matter how similarly they are cooked.

But I do have three ways to cook our country-cured hams, and I've never had a guest who didn't exclaim and usually ask that I record the steps from the ham house to the table. This puts me on the spot because sometimes I soak them overnight and sometimes I don't. Sometimes I bake them in the oven and sometimes I boil them on top of the stove. Often, I just shave off a 1/4-inch slice and fry it quickly and serve it with red-eye gravy.

Here are the three methods for cooking Talmadge Country-Cured Ham.

TALMADGE COUNTRY-CURED HAM
(*Do not overcook—slice thinner than commercial ham.*)

OVEN-BAKING METHOD

Wash ham thoroughly. Place in a large container filled with warm water and soak overnight. Drain. Place in roaster. Pour 2 pints of cola drink or fruit juice and an equal amount of water over ham. Cover with lid or foil. Bake in a 350° F. oven 20 minutes to the pound (approximately 4 hours for a 12-pound ham). Remove outer skin and cut off excess fat. Score remaining fat, insert cloves. Cover with brown sugar or a fruit glaze. Bake in hot oven (450° F.) for 20 minutes or until glazed or brown.

86

I was the unsalaried President, Secretary, Treasurer, Salesperson, Bookkeeper, Manager and Janitor!

TOP-OF-STOVE METHOD

Wash ham thoroughly, soak overnight, drain. Place ham in roasting pan in water to cover, along with 6 onions, 2 cups brown sugar, 1 pint vinegar, 2 bay leaves and 24 cloves. Cover and simmer (do not boil) 20 minutes to the pound. The ham is done when the small bone at the hock end can be twisted out. Let ham cool in liquid. Then remove skin and cut off excess fat, score and insert whole cloves. Glaze with mixture of 1 cup brown sugar and 2 teaspoons dry mustard. Bake 20 minutes at 450° F. to glaze.

COUNTRY FRYING METHOD

Cut slices ¼″ thick (very important). Lightly grease pan (bacon fat or lard). Fry on each side and remove from pan immediately. To hot fat remaining, add ¼ teaspoon sugar and 4 tablespoons water (or coffee). Cover pan and simmer a few more minutes to make red-eye gravy, adding paprika to make gravy redder if desired. Pour gravy over ham slices to serve.

Country ham, hot or cold, has several good companions which can be served for variation:

1. Horseradish mixed with whipped cream, in proportions to suit your own taste.

2. Lime gelatin, made according to the recipe on the package, with 2 tablespoons of horseradish added. Cut this in squares and serve on lettuce leaves.

3. Sweet Mustard Sauce, made as follows:

SWEET MUSTARD SAUCE

¼ *stick butter*	*2 teaspoons dry mustard*
2 teaspoons flour	*2 teaspoons sugar*
½ *cup milk*	*1 teaspoon vinegar*

Melt butter in double boiler over hot water. Blend in flour and milk. Dissolve mustard and sugar in vinegar and add to sauce, stirring until smooth and creamy and heated through.

2

Other Varieties of Ham

SMOKED PICNIC, smoked boneless and smoked hams (shank and butt portions) all should be baked on a rack, uncovered, in a 325° F. oven until a meat thermometer registers 170° F. internal temperature. A meat thermometer is helpful for best results. Insert the thermometer at an angle so the tip is in the center of the meat and not resting on fat or bone. If you do not have a meat thermometer, bake ham 25 minutes to the pound. Remove rind, score fat by cutting diagonal gashes across the ham in diamond shape, stud with cloves and add one of the glazes beginning on page 90. Bake 20 minutes longer.

The canned and processed hams are the easiest to prepare. Already tender, they require no soaking (unlike country-cured hams) and a shorter baking time than the preceding hams. As in the case of smoked picnic and other hams (except country-cured), don't add water, don't cover and don't baste. Place the ham in a slow oven (300° F.) and bake for 18 minutes per pound (internal temperature should reach 140° F.). One-half hour before baking time is over, remove ham, score and decorate, and return it to the oven for the last half-hour of baking.

HAM GLAZES AND SAUCES

Orange Glaze
Applesauce Glaze
Brown Sugar Glaze
Simple Plum Glaze

Pungent Plum Glaze
Fruit Sauce
Raisin Sauce

HAM RECIPES

Ham-Chicken Pinwheels
Ham with Broccoli
Glazed Canned Ham
Georgia Buck
Glazed Fresh Ham
Ham Loaf
Jellied Ham Loaf
Sweet and Sour Ham Loaf
Ham with Madeira and Onions
Cold Ham Mousse

Hot Ham Mousse
Sherry-Glazed Ham
Smothered Ham
Ham Soufflé
Ham Steak
Ham Steak with Cranberry Sauce
Ham and Yam Bake
Ham and Yam Loaf
Hamming It Up

HAM GLAZES AND SAUCES

Certain sauces, as well as glazes, go well with ham and pork, especially when the meat has been cooked on a grill or rotisserie. Some are mild, others hot or spicy—but none should mask the natural meat flavor. These sauces can be used as glazes to baste meat during cooking, or they may be served as an accompaniment. I like to use a small paintbrush for basting.

Jamie Wyeth introduced me to his pig at the Chadds Ford Museum.

Orange Glaze

1 cup brown sugar	*1 tablespoon vinegar*
1 tablespoon flour	*3 tablespoons frozen concentrated*
1 teaspoon dry mustard	*orange juice*

Combine all ingredients, stirring until smooth. Add to baking ham about 30 minutes before ham is done, first decorating ham with cloves. Return to oven to finish cooking and to set glaze. Enough for a 14-pound ham.

Applesauce Glaze

1 cup applesauce
*3 tablespoons small cinnamon
   candies*
¼ teaspoon powdered ginger
2 tablespoons lemon juice

Combine first 3 ingredients. Cook slowly, stirring occasionally until candies are melted. Stir in lemon juice. Use to baste ham during last 20 to 30 minutes of baking. Enough for a 14-pound ham.

Brown Sugar Glaze

1 cup brown sugar
2 tablespoons flour
½ teaspoon dry mustard
1 teaspoon ground cloves
¼ cup vinegar

Mix together all ingredients. Brush glaze on meat during last 20 to 30 minutes of baking.

Simple Plum Glaze

*1 large can (1 pound 14 ounces)
   plums, pitted*
*¼ cup frozen concentrated
   orange juice*
½ teaspoon Worcestershire sauce

Drain plums, reserving ¾ cup juice. Force plums through sieve. Add the reserved plum juice, the orange juice and the Worcestershire sauce to sieved plums. Mix well. Brush meat with glaze during last 20 to 30 minutes of baking.

Pungent Plum Sauce

1 can (17 ounces) purple plums   *⅛ teaspoon allspice*
3 tablespoons cornstarch   *1 tablespoon butter*
¼ teaspoon cinnamon   *2 tablespoons lemon juice*
½ teaspoon salt

Drain plums, cut each in half and remove pits. Reserve liquid. Combine cornstarch, cinnamon, salt and allspice. Add to plum syrup and stir well. Cook, stirring constantly, until thickened and clear. Add plum halves, butter and lemon juice. Heat thoroughly. Use either as glaze or sauce. Enough for a 14-pound ham.

Fruit Sauce

In a saucepan, mix well ½ cup light molasses, ⅔ cup apricot preserves, 2 tablespoons slivered orange peel, 2 tablespoons slivered lemon peel and ⅔ cup port wine or orange juice. Simmer for 5 minutes. Baste meat, reserving most of sauce to serve hot over meat slices.

Raisin Sauce

1 cup sugar   *⅛ teaspoon pepper*
½ cup water   *½ teaspoon salt*
1 cup raisins   *¼ teaspoon cloves*
2 tablespoons butter   *1 8-ounce jar currant jelly*
3 tablespoons vinegar

Mix first 8 ingredients together and boil 5 minutes. Add currant jelly and cook, stirring until it is dissolved. Serve as accompaniment to baked or boiled ham.

HAM RECIPES

Ham-Chicken Pinwheels

2 *whole chicken breasts, skinned*
   and boned
⅛ *teaspoon dried basil leaves,*
   crushed
⅛ *teaspoon salt*
   freshly ground pepper

⅛ *teaspoon garlic salt*
4 *thin slices cooked ham*
2 *teaspoons lemon juice*
   paprika
   butter

Cut chicken breasts in half, arrange on board and pound to ⅓-inch thickness. Combine basil, salt, pepper, garlic salt; sprinkle on chicken. Place a slice of ham on each chicken breast; roll lengthwise with ham inside. There will be 4 rolls. Place rolls, seam side down, in buttered baking dish. Sprinkle with lemon juice; add a few dashes of paprika. Dot with butter. Bake at 350° F. for 35 to 40 minutes. Chill; cut into ¼-inch slices. Makes about 32 slices.

Ham with Broccoli

1 *pound broccoli*
8 *to 10 slices boiled or baked ham*
4 *tablespoons sherry*

2 *cups Basic Cream Sauce*
   (p. 26)
4 *tablespoons Parmesan cheese*

Cook broccoli until just tender. In a baking dish, arrange a layer of broccoli, then a layer of ham. Pour sherry evenly over ham and broccoli. Add half the Parmesan cheese to the cream sauce; pour over ham and broccoli. Sprinkle top with remaining Parmesan cheese. If main ingredients are warm when combined, you need only brown under broiler until bubbly. Otherwise, bake in 350° F. oven for 10 minutes before browning under broiler. Serves 4.

Glazed Canned Ham

1 canned ham (5 pounds)
  whole cloves
½ cup light molasses
½ cup seasoned dry bread crumbs

Score top of the ham into diamonds with a sharp knife. Push a whole clove into the center of each diamond. Place ham on a rack in a foil-lined shallow roasting pan. Brush with a thin coating of molasses. Roast in a preheated oven (350° F.) for 1 hour. Brush ham with molasses a few times during baking, saving some to mix with crumbs later. Remove ham from oven and raise oven temperature to 400° F.

  Mix remaining molasses with ¼ cup of the crumbs. Spread this mixture around cloves on top of ham. Sprinkle with remaining crumbs. Return to oven and roast 20 to 25 minutes more until top is golden brown. Serve with Fruit Sauce (p. 93), or any of the sauces in the preceding section. Serves 6 to 8.

Georgia Buck

This is one of the first recipes we used on the Talmadge Country-Cured Ham package. It is prepared by placing one slice of fried country ham on a toasted English muffin, topped with a poached egg and covered with Blender Hollandaise Sauce (p. 26) or a slice of cheese. Run it under the broiler to serve bubbly hot.

Glazed Fresh Ham

(*Rotisserie*)

10-pound fresh ham
  salt
¼ cup currant jelly
3 drops Tabasco sauce
⅛ teaspoon ground ginger
⅛ teaspoon ground cloves

Insert rotisserie rod through center of ham. Season with salt and place on rotisserie. Insert meat thermometer. Roast at low to moderate temperature (325° F. to 350° F.) until meat thermometer registers 170° F., usually 3½ to 4½ hours. In a saucepan combine jelly, Tabasco sauce, ginger and cloves. Heat to boiling, stirring constantly. During last 30 minutes of roasting time, brush occasionally with jelly mixture. Serves 16 to 20.

Ham Loaf

1 pound lean ham	*6 saltine crackers rolled fine*
½ pound lean beef	*1 bell pepper chopped fine*
½ pound fresh pork	*¼ cup milk*
2 eggs, slightly beaten	*few sprigs of parsley*
2 tablespoons Worcestershire Sauce	*freshly ground pepper*

Ask your butcher to grind meats coarsely. Combine all ingredients and mix well. Shape into loaf and put in greased baking dish. Bake at 350° F. for 1 hour. Serves 4.

Jellied Ham Loaf

1 smoked picnic shoulder	*1 tablespoon prepared mustard*
3 cups ham stock	*2 envelopes unflavored gelatin*
1 tablespoon prepared horseradish	*½ cup cold water*
	3 bouillon cubes

Simmer picnic shoulder in hot water for about 2 hours. Cool in stock; reserve 3 cups of stock. Grind meat in food chopper, using coarse blade. You will need 5 cups of ground ham. Add horseradish and mustard; mix well. Soak gelatin in cold water until softened. Add to 3 cups of heated stock in which 3 bouillon cubes have been dissolved. Combine gelatin-stock mixture with ground ham and pack into an attractive bowl or mold. Chill until firm. Garnish with hard-boiled eggs which have been pressed through a sieve. Serves 6 to 8.

Sweet-and-Sour Ham Loaf

1½ pounds ground ham　　*1 cup bread crumbs*
1½ pounds ground pork　　*1 cup milk*
　2 eggs

Grind meats together or have butcher do this. Combine with other ingredients and shape into a loaf in a loaf pan or casserole. Pour half of the Sweet-and-Sour Sauce below over the loaf and bake for 1 hour at 350° F. Cover with remaining sauce before serving. Serves 6.

SWEET-AND-SOUR SAUCE
1½ cups brown sugar　　*½ cup cider vinegar*
　½ cup water　　　　　*1 teaspoon dry mustard*

Combine ingredients and mix well. Cook over low heat, stirring occasionally, until syrupy and flavors well blended. Keep warm. Use as directed above.

Ham with Madeira and Onions

　3- pound ham slice, center cut　　*1 pound small white onions*
1¼ cup Madeira　　　　　　　　*½ cup slivered almonds or*
　½ teaspoon dry mustard　　　　　*peanuts or pecans*
　½ cup (generous) light-brown　　*1 tablespoon butter*
　　sugar

Pour wine over ham slice. Let stand at room temperature for 1 hour. Preheat oven to 350° F. Bake ham (with Madeira in which it was marinating) for 20 minutes. Blend mustard with brown sugar. Remove ham from oven.

Spread sugar mixture over ham, packing it down firmly. Surround with the onions. Return ham to oven and bake for 1 hour and 10 minutes, basting onions and ham every 20 minutes or so with pan liquid. Add more wine if necessary. Sauté nuts in butter, stirring, until lightly browned. Drain on paper towels. Sprinkle over ham and onions when ready to serve. Serves 6 generously.

Cold Ham Mousse

2 *envelopes unflavored gelatin*	¾ *cup finely chopped celery*
½ *cup cold water*	¼ *cup chopped bell pepper*
1 *can mushroom soup*	4 *cups finely chopped or ground*
¼ *cup ketchup*	*boiled or baked ham*
¼ *teaspoon Worcestershire sauce*	¾ *cup mayonnaise*
1 *teaspoon prepared mustard*	*salt and pepper to taste*
½ *teaspoon scraped onion*	

Soften gelatin in cold water. Heat soup slowly to boiling point. Add gelatin mixture to soup to dissolve. Blend ketchup, Worcestershire sauce, mustard, onion, celery, pepper and ham. Add to gelatin-soup mixture and stir until blended. Fold in mayonnaise. Salt and pepper to taste. Place in attractive mold or other deep dish. Chill until set. Serves 8 to 10.

Hot Ham Mousse

4 *tablespoons butter*	*paprika to taste*
4 *tablespoons flour*	1 *teaspoon lemon juice*
1 *cup milk*	1 *cup ground country ham*
½ *teaspoon salt*	3 *eggs, separated*

Make a cream sauce of the butter, flour and milk. Add salt, paprika and lemon juice. Add ham and beaten egg yolks. When cool, fold in stiffly beaten egg whites and pour into a buttered casserole. Bake at 400° F. for 20 to 25 minutes. Serves 4.

Sherry-Glazed Ham

1 *8- to 10-pound canned ham*	*dash of nutmeg*
1½ *cups cream sherry*	½ *cup honey*
½ *cup apricot or peach jam*	1 *teaspoon cornstarch*

Place ham in shallow pan. Pour ½ cup sherry over. Bake at 325° F. for

1 hour. Combine jam with nutmeg and honey; stir in cornstarch. Add remaining sherry. Cook, stirring, until thickened. Spoon over ham. Bake for 20 minutes longer or until glazed. Serves 16 to 20.

Smothered Ham

1 13- to 15-pound fully cooked
ham
2 tablespoons prepared mustard
½ cup red currant jelly
¼ cup light brown sugar

3 cups finely rolled salted cracker
crumbs
6 tablespoons melted butter or
margarine

Preheat oven to 325° F. Place ham, fat side up, on rack in shallow roasting pan. Bake for 2 hours. Take ham out of oven and remove rind and all but a thin layer of fat. In a small saucepan, heat mustard, currant jelly and brown sugar, stirring until smooth. Spread over ham. Combine cracker crumbs and melted butter. Pack onto ham. Return to a 425° F. oven and bake until crust is lightly browned. Serves 16 to 20.

Ham Soufflé

2 cups milk
1 tablespoon butter
⅓ cup cornmeal
1 cup grated cheese

3 eggs, separated
1 teaspoon mustard
salt, pepper, paprika to taste
1 cup ground cooked ham

Combine milk, butter, cornmeal in double boiler. Add cheese and stir until melted. Beat yolks and add mustard, salt, pepper, paprika. Combine with hot cornmeal mixture and add the ground ham. Beat egg whites until stiff and fold into ham mixture. Pour into greased 1- to 1½-quart casserole. Bake at 350° F. for 40 minutes. Serves 5 or 6.

Ham Steak

1 large center cut precooked ham   *prepared mustard*
*   steak 1½ to 2 inches thick*   *brown sugar*

Spread mustard smoothly over both sides of ham steak. Sprinkle generously with brown sugar. Run under broiler until bubbly and slightly brown. One steak serves 2 to 3.

Ham Steak with Cranberry Sauce

1 ham steak 1 inch thick   *1 tablespoon prepared*
1 cup whole-cranberry sauce   * horseradish*
1 tablespoon grated orange rind   *¼ cup coarsely chopped pecans*

Place ham steak on rack in roasting pan. Combine cranberry sauce, orange rind, horseradish, pecans. Spread on top of ham. Bake at 325° F. for 45 minutes. Serves 2 or 3.

Ham and Yam Bake

2 slices cooked, sugar-cured ham,   *4 tablespoons brown sugar*
*   ¾ inch thick*   *1 tablespoon dry mustard*
1 small can sliced pineapple   *½ teaspoon black pepper*
*   (reserve juice)*
1 (29-ounce) can sweet potatoes
*   (or bake 4 large sweet*
*   potatoes in advance, peel and*
*   cut in half before placing*
*   around ham)*

Place ham in a shallow broiling pan or flat casserole. Arrange pineapple on ham. Place potatoes around ham. Mix reserved pineapple juice with brown sugar, mustard and pepper, pour over ham and bake at 350° F. for 1 hour or until ham and potatoes are heated through. Serves 4 to 6.

Ham and Yam Loaf

2 *pounds lean ham or pork*
  shoulder, ground
1 *pound veal, ground*
1 *egg, beaten*

2 *slices bread, crumbled and*
  moistened with water
⅛ *teaspoon black pepper*
⅓ *cup finely diced celery*

Combine all ingredients and shape into loaf. Bake for 1½ hours at 350° F. During the last 10 minutes the ham is baking, combine the following ingredients:

1 *can (1 pound) sweet potatoes,*
  heated, drained, mashed
½ *stick butter or margarine,*
  melted

¼ *teaspoon salt*
3 *tablespoons sugar*
⅓ *cup drained crushed*
  pineapple

Mash all ingredients together thoroughly. (I make this "icing" in my mixer—the beaters will remove any "strings" from potatoes.) Remove loaf from oven. Turn oven up to 400° F. Spread the "icing" over the loaf and return to oven for 5 to 10 minutes. Serves 6.

Hamming It Up

There are many ways to use leftover ham, but the one my friend Yolande Gwin, an Atlanta author and news columnist, concocted is quick and easy.

Cook 1 cup quick-cooking rice according to directions. When nearly ready to serve, add 2 cups diced cooked ham, 6 sliced stuffed olives, a small jar of chopped pimientos and 1 tablespoon butter. Cover. When all liquid has evaporated, sprinkle with soy sauce and serve.

With a side dish of sliced tomatoes and some French-cut green beans, this is a meal enough for two.

3

Pork Roasts,
Pork Chops,
Spareribs, Bacon

THE VARIETY OF PORK PRODUCTS for preparing in the kitchen or on the outdoor grill can add zest to meal planning. Now produced to contain less fat and fewer calories, pork can and should be included in every diet for people who are concerned about weight control.

Pork roasts, like most hams, should be placed fat side up on a rack in an open roasting pan. Do not add water and do not cover. Roast in a 325° F. oven until the meat thermometer registers 170° F., allowing approximately 30 to 40 minutes per pound. (See Tables on Pork Cookery, page 248.)

The lower internal cooking temperature necessary for these modern pork products requires less cooking time. There is less shrinkage and loss of moisture.

A quick list of what is available at your market's meat counter includes:

Pork roasts, fresh or smoked

Spareribs, back ribs and country-style backbones

Chops and pork steaks, including loin and rib chops, fresh and smoked, butterfly chops, and chops with a pocket for stuffing

Sliced Canadian-style bacon

Fresh and smoked hocks

This is by no means a complete list. The Pig'lossary on page 124 lists other pork delectables.

PORK RECIPES

Pork Loin Roast
Pork Loin in Milk with
   Lemon and Orange Slices
Pork Steak (Shoulder Slices)
Pork Steaks with Apple Kraut
Cola Pork Steaks
Party Pork Roast
Grilled Porkburgers
Grilled Pork Loin
Pork Tenderloin Patties
Pork Tenderloin Casserole
Smoked Pork Shoulder with
   Horseradish Sauce
Smoked Pork Shoulder Roll with
   Apricot Glaze
Pork Chops with Dumplings

Pork Chops with Peaches
Stuffed Pork Chops
Apple-Peanut Stuffing
Apple-Raisin Stuffing
Floured Pork Chops
Pork Chops Turner County Style
Pork Chops with Vegetables
Broiled Pork Chops with
   Apple Ring Fritters
Pork Rice Skillet
Barbecued Spareribs
Citrus Glaze for Spareribs
Charcoal-Grilled Back Ribs with
   Apricot Glaze
Bacon, Tomatoes and Rice
Saw Mill "Chicken"

Pork Loin Roast

Choose a roast of size appropriate for your family or party (allow ⅓ to ½ pound per person). Have fat trimmed. Place roast, fat side up, on rack in a shallow roasting pan. Insert meat thermometer in thickest part of roast, avoiding bone. Do not add water. Roast uncovered in 325° F. oven until thermometer registers 170 °F. For a 4- to 6-pound roast allow 2½ to 3½ hours for roasting (30 to 40 minutes per pound). Serve plain or with one of the glazes beginning on page 90. Add glaze during last 30 minutes of roasting.

Pork Loin in Milk with
Lemon and Orange Slices

1 4-pound pork loin
4 tablespoons butter or
  margarine
4 tablespoons vegetable oil

freshly ground black pepper
salt to taste
4 cups milk

Make sure pork loin is carefully trimmed of excess fat. In a heavy pot or casserole, heat butter (or margarine) and oil until bubbly. Add pork loin and brown well on all sides. Season. Add milk. Cook 3 to 4 hours over medium heat on top of stove, turning occasionally. Keep lid on pot, slightly ajar. Remove meat and slice. Skim fat from liquid. The milk will have turned to semi-congealed globules, and will be an excellent sauce. Serve with Lemon and Orange Slices (below). Serves 6 to 8.

LEMON AND ORANGE SLICES
4 oranges (navels are best)
2 lemons (rind of 2, juice of 1)

½ cup brown sugar or honey
½ cup orange juice

Peel oranges and slice very thin. Arrange 1 layer of slices in decorative serving dish. Grate lemon rind. Sprinkle half the rind over orange slices. Add half the brown sugar or honey. Arrange another layer of orange slices over the first. Add the remainder of the lemon rind and sugar or honey. Pour the orange and lemon juice over the whole. Refrigerate overnight, turning a few times if possible.

Pork Steak (Shoulder Slices)

4 pork steaks from shoulder,
  ¾ inch thick
salt to taste
freshly ground pepper
fat for browning

4 slices onion
⅓ cup water
4 slices tomato
4 green pepper rings

Season steaks with salt and pepper. Brown quickly in whatever fat you are using. Pour off excess. Place a slice of onion on top of each pork steak. Add water. Cover and simmer 45 minutes. Add a slice of tomato and a slice of green pepper to each pork steak. Cover and simmer 15 minutes longer. Serves 4.

Pork Steaks with Apple Kraut

4 *pork shoulder steaks*
2 *tablespoons bacon drippings*
  salt
  freshly ground pepper
1 *tablespoon prepared mustard*
1 *tablespoon prepared*
  horseradish

1 *can (1 pound 13 ounces)*
  sauerkraut, drained
2 *medium apples, chopped*
½ *cup chopped onion*
1 *teaspoon caraway seeds*

Brown steaks in drippings. Pour off excess. Season with salt and pepper. Combine mustard and horseradish and spread over steaks. Combine sauerkraut, apples, onion and caraway seeds in a baking dish. Arrange steaks on top. Cover well. Bake at 350° F. for 30 minutes. Uncover and bake for 30 minutes more. Serves 4.

Cola Pork Steaks

1 *can cola drink*
3 *cloves garlic, minced*

1 *cup soy sauce*
6 *pork shoulder steaks*

Mix cola, minced garlic, and soy sauce; pour over steaks. Marinate in refrigerator for several hours. Bake at 325° F. for 1 hour, basting frequently with marinade. Serves 6.

Party Pork Roast

6-*pound pork roast*   *salt and freshly ground pepper*

Have butcher remove backbone and form pork loin into crown roast. Tie so rib bones are exposed. Preheat oven to 325° F. Season pork with salt and pepper to taste. Place roast rib side down on rack. Roast un-covered for 2 hours or until meat thermometer reaches 170° F. Slice between ribs to serve, 1 rib per person. Serves 10.

Grilled Porkburgers

Because of their healthful qualities, I like to serve Pork-burgers sometimes when my grandchildren visit the farm. Try this recipe on the outdoor grill:

1 *pound ground pork (shoulder cut is a good, lean cut)*

¼ *cup Country Barbecue Sauce (p. 40) or store-purchased*

¼ *teaspoon monosodium glutamate (optional)*

¼ *teaspoon salt*

Mix all ingredients and form 4 patties. Over a medium heat, brown on one side; turn and continue broiling until done. Allow 20 minutes' cooking time. (Porkburgers may be broiled in the kitchen range, too, of course.) Serves 4.

Grilled Pork Loin

Another pork dish for the outdoor grill, popular for in-formal parties with 8 to 10 guests, is Grilled Pork Loin. You can use a rotisserie or, if your grill doesn't have one, just put it on the grate and turn and baste frequently.

1 *5-pound pork loin, boned and rolled*

1 *quart Country Barbecue Sauce (p. 40)*

6 *large white onions, sliced*

2 *loaves rye bread, hand-sliced 1 inch thick*

1 *dozen dill pickles, sliced*

Heat grill. Put roast on spit or directly on grill. If pork is to be done on the spit, baste with sauce from time to time as it turns. If to be roasted directly on grill, turn to brown all sides evenly, brushing with sauce as necessary. Watch carefully to see that it doesn't burn, regulat-ing heat or its distance from the heat, depending on the type of grill. Count on using 1 pint of sauce for basting and keep remaining pint of sauce hot. Allow for 3 hours' roasting time—meat thermometer should register 170° F.

On each plate place 1 slice bread and a few onion and pickle slices. Place a thick slice of pork on bread and spoon sauce over (or guests can serve themselves). A tossed salad and dessert are all you need for a complete informal party meal. Serves 10.

Pork Tenderloin Patties

1½ pounds pork tenderloin	*3 tablespoons bacon drippings*
1 egg, beaten	*6 orange slices, cut 1 inch thick*
salt	*6 thin slices of onion*
¾ cup very fine cracker crumbs	*¼ cup water*

Have your butcher grind the pork tenderloin. Shape into 6 patties. Dip patties in egg with salt; coat with cracker crumbs. Brown slowly in drippings. Arrange an orange slice and onion slice on each patty. Add water, cover tightly and cook slowly for ½ hour. Serves 6.

Pork Tenderloin Casserole

1½ pounds pork tenderloin	*1 cup chopped pecans*
3 tablespoons bacon drippings	*¼ cup finely chopped onion*
salt	*½ cup chopped celery*
freshly ground pepper	*3 tablespoons soy sauce*
¼ teaspoon garlic salt	*¼ teaspoon ginger*
2 cups cooked rice	

Have your butcher grind the pork tenderloin. Shape into 6 patties. Brown patties in drippings. Season with salt, pepper and garlic salt. Combine rice, nuts, onion, celery, soy sauce and ginger. Pour into greased baking dish. Place patties on top. Cover tightly and bake at 350° F. for 45 minutes. Serves 6.

Smoked Pork Shoulder with Horseradish Sauce

3 *pounds smoked pork shoulder*	½ *cup brown sugar*
water	1 *tablespoon flour*
½ *teaspoon cinnamon*	½ *teaspoon dry mustard*
½ *teaspoon celery seed*	⅛ *teaspoon ground cloves*
6 *whole cloves*	2 *tablespoons apricot, peach or*
1 *medium onion, sliced*	*apple juice*
1 *bay leaf crumbled*	

Simmer meat, tightly covered, for 2 hours in water barely to cover, to which cinnamon, celery seed, cloves, onion and bay leaf have been added. Remove from liquid. Place meat on rack in roasting pan. Mix brown sugar, flour, mustard, cloves and either apricot, peach or apple juice. Spread mixture on meat. Bake at 350° F. for 30 minutes. Serve with Horseradish Sauce, below. Serves 6 to 8.

HORSERADISH SAUCE

3 *tablespoons butter*	2 *cups milk*
3 *tablespoons flour*	3 *tablespoons prepared*
salt to taste	*horseradish*
½ *teaspoon onion salt*	½ *cup dairy sour cream*

Melt butter, stir in flour, salt and onion salt. Add milk gradually. Stir constantly over medium heat until thick. Remove from heat. Add horseradish. Cool. Fold in sour cream. Makes 3 cups.

Smoked Pork Shoulder Roll with Apricot Glaze

2- to 3-*pound pork shoulder roll*	¼ *teaspoon dry mustard*
(*butt*)	¼ *teaspoon grated orange rind*
⅓ *cup apricot preserves*	

Place smoked shoulder roll on rack in a roasting pan. Insert meat thermometer. Do not add water. Roast uncovered in a 325° F. oven until thermometer registers 170° F. Allow 35 to 40 minutes per pound for roasting. Combine preserves, mustard, and orange rind. Spread mixture over meat the last 20 minutes to glaze. Serves 4 to 6.

Pork Chops with Dumplings

8 pork chops, trimmed of fat   *1 large onion, sliced*
3 cups water

Brown chops in a heavy skillet. Add 1 cup of water and the onion. Cover and simmer 45 minutes. Spoon as much fat from liquid as possible. Add 2 cups water and prepare Dumplings, below.

DUMPLINGS
2 cups all-purpose flour   *1 cup milk*

Mix flour and milk well. Drop with spoon onto chops in simmering liquid. Cook uncovered for 10 minutes. Cover and cook another 10 minutes. Serves 8.

Pork Chops with Peaches

6 pork chops, 1 inch thick   *2 tablespoons honey*
2 tablespoons bacon drippings   *1 teaspoon lemon juice*
   salt   *¼ teaspoon cinnamon*
   freshly ground pepper   *⅛ teaspoon ginger*
1 large can sliced cling peaches   *flour for gravy*

Brown chops in drippings. Pour off fat. Season chops with salt and pepper. Drain peaches, reserving juice. Combine peach juice, honey, lemon juice, cinnamon and ginger. Pour over chops. Cover tightly and cook for 1 hour. Add peach slices. Cook until heated through. Remove chops. Thicken liquid with flour (1 tablespoon to 1 cup liquid) and spoon over chops. Serves 6.

Stuffed Pork Chops

Pork chops become very special when suffed with any of several tasty mixtures. Try these with either Apple-Peanut or Apple-Raisin Stuffing, below. Have your butcher cut a pocket in each of 6 pork chops cut 1 inch thick. Stuff with desired mixture. Close pocket with toothpicks. Season chops with salt and pepper and brown in bacon drippings or other fat. Arrange chops in casserole. Pour liquid over as directed in stuffing recipes below. Cover and bake for 1 hour at 325° F. Serves 6.

APPLE-PEANUT STUFFING

¾ *cup chopped apples*
¼ *cup chopped peanuts*
2 *tablespoons brown sugar*

1½ *cups ginger ale*
3 *tablespoons tomato paste*

Combine apples with peanuts and brown sugar. Stuff pork chops with mixture and close with toothpicks. Mix ginger ale with tomato paste and pour over chops. Bake as directed above.

APPLE-RAISIN STUFFING

¼ *cup milk*
1 *cup bread crumbs*
  pinch of salt
1 *teaspoon sage*

1 *cup chopped apple*
½ *cup raisins*
1 *tablespoon butter*
1 *cup apple juice*

Pour milk over bread crumbs. Add salt, sage, apple, raisins and melted butter. Stuff each chop with ¼ cup of apple mixture. Fasten with toothpicks. Brown, then bake in casserole as directed in Stuffed Pork Chops recipe above, first pouring apple juice over chops.

Floured Pork Chops

6 *pork chops*
  flour
  salt

pepper
shortening

Roll pork chops in mixture of flour, salt and pepper. Reserve a little of the flour mixture to make gravy later. Brown chops in shortening and sauté slowly until done. Keep chops warm.

To make gravy: Blend 3 tablespoons of leftover flour mixture with approximately the same amount of fat left in pan in which chops were cooked. Add 2 cups water, or broth, or a mixture of both, and stir constantly until thickened. Pour over chops or serve separately. Serves 6.

Pork Chops Turner County Style

4 *large sweet potatoes*
1 *large orange*
¾ *cup brown sugar*

4 *pork chops*
salt and pepper to taste
3 *tablespoons water*

Wash, then cook, sweet potatoes in salted boiling water until tender. Cool, skin and slice into ½-inch rounds. Slice orange, unpeeled, very thin and remove seeds. Arrange a layer of sweet potatoes and sliced orange in buttered casserole. Sprinkle with the sugar. Season pork chops with salt and pepper and brown in a skillet. Place on top of potatoes, add 3 tablespoons of water, cover and bake for 1 hour in 350° oven. Baste occasionally with juices in casserole. Serves 4.

Pork Chops with Vegetables

8 *pork chops*
8 *tablespoons raw rice*
2 *cups sliced carrots*
2 *tablespoons onion*

2 *cups diced celery*
2 *cups tomato juice*
salt and pepper to taste

Sear pork chops in small amount of fat, then arrange in a casserole. Sprinkle raw rice over chops, add raw vegetables. Pour tomato juice over all. Salt and pepper to taste. Cover and bake in 350° F. oven for 50 minutes to 1 hour. Serves 8.

Broiled Pork Chops with Apple Ring Fritters

6 pork chops, cut 1 to 1½ inches   *salt and pepper to taste*
thick

Place pork chops on rack in broiler pan. Insert pan so tops of chops are about 5 inches from heat. Broil 5 minutes, turn and broil 8 minutes longer. Continue broiling about 15 to 20 minutes longer, turning at least twice. Season with salt and pepper. Serve with Apple Ring Fritters, below.

Apple Ring Fritters

4 medium-sized tart apples   *½ cup milk*
1½ cups flour   *¼ cup sugar*
2 tablespoons sugar   *1 teaspoon cinnamon*
¼ teaspoon salt   *lard for frying*
2 eggs, separated

Pare and core apples. Cut into crosswise slices about ¼ inch thick. Sift together flour, the 2 tablespoons sugar, and salt. Beat together egg yolks and milk. Beat egg whites until stiff. Stir egg-yolk mixture into dry ingredients, mixing until smooth. Fold egg whites into mixture. Combine ¼ cup sugar and cinnamon. Coat apple slices with cinnamon sugar and dip into batter. Coat thoroughly with batter. Fry in hot lard until golden brown. Serve hot. Serves 6.

Pork-Rice Skillet

1 pound boneless pork, cut in   *1 can (4 ounces) mushrooms*
¾-inch cubes   *with their liquid*
½ cup diced green pepper   *2¼ cups water*
bacon drippings   *2 teaspoons salt*
1 cup Basic Cream Sauce (p. 26)   *½ teaspoon sage*

1 cup rice	*¼ cup coarsely chopped*
1 cup chopped celery	*pimiento*

Brown pork and green pepper in bacon drippings in 12-inch skillet; drain. Stir in cream sauce, mushrooms, water, salt and sage. Bring to boil. Reduce heat, cover and cook over low heat for 20 minutes. Remove cover, stir in rice and celery. Cover and continue cooking about 25 minutes. Stir occasionally. Add pimiento just before serving. Serves 4 to 6.

Barbecued Spareribs

Have your butcher saw across rib bones. Allow at least ⅔ pound ribs per person. I always boil spareribs for at least 15 minutes before preparing to roast them. This removes excess fat. Drain ribs and brush them generously with Country Barbecue Sauce (p. 40) or with Citrus Glaze (below). Roast tightly covered in 350° F. oven for 1 hour. Uncover, turn, baste again with barbecue sauce, and roast another 30 minutes or until brown.

To cook on a rotisserie, allow 2 hours, basting frequently with barbecue sauce or glaze. To grill over charcoal, allow 2 hours, turning 3 or 4 times.

Citrus Glaze for Spareribs

1 cup Country Barbecue Sauce	*2 tablespoons soy sauce*
(p. 40)	*2 tablespoons minced onion*
1 cup fresh orange juice	*1½ teaspoons salt*
⅓ cup fresh lemon juice	*1 tablespoon grated orange peel*
½ cup brown sugar	

Combine all ingredients. Place ribs on grill and apply generous amounts of glaze throughout the cooking process. This is ample sauce for 6 pounds of ribs.

Charcoal-Grilled Back Ribs with Apricot Glaze

4 pounds pork back ribs, separated.

After charcoal has burned until coals are gray, place pork, rib ends down, on grill. Grill for 2 hours, turning frequently and basting with Apricot Glaze (below). Serves 4.

APRICOT GLAZE

½ *cup apricot preserves*   *salt*
1½ *tablespoons lemon juice*   *freshly ground pepper*
2 *teaspoons mustard*

Mix all ingredients well and use as basting sauce for ribs.

Bacon, Tomatoes and Rice

5 *slices breakfast bacon*   3 *cups cooked rice*
½ *cup chopped onion*   *salt to taste*
½ *cup chopped green pepper*   *freshly ground black pepper*
3 *large tomatoes cut into small*
   pieces

Cook bacon until crisp. Drain. Pour off all but 3 tablespoons drippings. Add onion and green pepper to skillet and cook until tender. Add tomatoes, rice and crumbled bacon. Season. Heat thoroughly. Serves 6 to 8.

Saw Mill "Chicken"

Fried country bacon—or fried "streak o' lean"—is one of Herman's favorite breakfast dishes. 'Cile usually just dips the country bacon in flour and fries it in hot fat as quickly as possible. More "refined" bacon can be dipped in the following batter:

½ *cup flour*   ¼ *teaspoon black pepper*
½ *cup milk*

Dip the bacon in batter made by beating together the above ingredients. Dust in plain flour and fry in small amount of grease at a low temperature until crisp and brown.

A traveler in the 1830's described a meal offered him near Columbus, Georgia, which, with the possible exception of the milk, probably represented the usual fare:

In the middle of the table was placed a bottle of whiskey, of which both host and hostess partook in no measured quantity, before they tasted any of the dishes. Pigs' feet pickled in vinegar formed the first course; then followed bacon with molasses; and the repast concluded with a super-abundance of milk and bread, which the landlord, to use his own expression, washed down with a half a tumbler of whiskey. The landlady, a real Amazon, was not a little surprised to see a person refusing such a delicacy as bacon swimming in molasses.

—*from* Hog Meat and Hoecake, *Food Supply in the Old South, 1840–1860, by Sam Bowers Hilliard, Southern Illinois University Press, Carbondale, 1972.*

4

Sausage

The sausage is as old as sin—and just as delightful.
—John Drury

JOHN DRURY, in his book entitled *Rare and Well Done—Some Historical Notes on Meats and Meatmen,* points out that the word "sausage" comes originally from *salsus,* a Latin word meaning "salted" (or preserved) meat. "As may be seen," says Drury, "the Latin origin of 'sausage' clearly indicates the great antiquity of this form of processed food. In fact, further research showed me that although the origin of sausage is clothed in mystery it has been with us since the dawn of history."*

The celebrated Greek poet Aristophanes, in his play *The Clouds,* written in 423 B.C., has one of his characters exclaim: "Let them make sausages of me and serve me up to the students."

I'm no historian, but I do have a saying that dates back in time that I frequently quote: "If you love the law and you love good sausage, don't watch either of them being made!" I've watched enough of both to realize the full meaning of that proverb.

Actually, homemade sausage isn't too difficult for anyone to make. You don't have to use casings. Simply grind the meat up and make either small rolls or patties.

* *Rare and Well Done,* p. 44.

SAUSAGE RECIPES

Talmadge Farm Pork Sausage
(*Mild*)

Don't ever let anyone tell you to make lean *sausage. Fat is an important ingredient and it takes a certain amount of fat to make good sausage—at least 40 to 45 percent fat.*

100 pounds of pork, first chopped
       into 1 inch cubes
 22 ounces salt
  3 ounces ground black pepper
       (medium grind)

  3 ounces rubbed sage
  1 ounce ground red pepper
  1 ounce crushed red pepper
  2 ounces light-brown sugar

After adding all seasoning, put meat through a grinder, using as sharp a blade as possible so the fat is not crushed. While working, keep it *cold* (temperature should be as close to 34° as possible). Freeze in rolls, patties or loaves of suitable size for your family.

Talmadge Farm Pork Sausage
(*Hot*)

Use same ingredients and instructions as above, adding 2 more ounces of ground red pepper.

Homemade Sausage #1

*1 pound lean pork (shoulder is
  a good cut for sausage)*
*½ pound bacon (to provide the
  fat to make good sausage)*
½ pound veal (optional)
1 teaspoon thyme

1 teaspoon rosemary
2 teaspoons sage
*¼ teaspoon cayenne pepper (or
  hot red pepper)*
1 teaspoon salt

Combine all ingredients and grind. You may need to add a small amount of water as you knead it lightly with your hands. Form patties or use as desired.

Homemade Sausage #2

3 pounds lean pork, ground twice
2 pounds pork fat, ground twice
1 clove garlic, mashed
1 teaspoon onion salt
1 teaspoon salt
2 teaspoons black pepper

1 tablespoon rubbed sage
1 teaspoon ground cloves
1 teaspoon mace
1 tablespoon minced parsley
1 bay leaf, crushed
¼ teaspoon ground allspice

Mix pork and pork fat well with all the other ingredients. Form patties or use as you would any sausage. Freeze for future use.

Sausage and Corn

1 pound sausage
4 eggs
1 cup bread crumbs
1 can (16 ounces) cream-style corn

*salt and coarsely ground
  pepper*
½ cup cracker crumbs

Combine sausage with beaten eggs, bread crumbs, corn and seasoning. Place in 2½ quart casserole. Top with cracker crumbs. Bake uncovered at 325° F. for 1 hour. Serves 6.

Country Sausage with Apples

4 cups green apples, peeled and
   sliced
½ cup butter

2 cups sugar
1½ pounds fresh pork sausage

Place apples, butter and sugar in heavy skillet and cook over low heat until sugar melts and apples are glazed well. Stir occasionally. Shape ground sausage into 3-inch patties and, using another skillet, brown them over low heat. Cook until done. Serve with glazed apples. Serves 4 to 6.

Pork Sausage and English Muffins

1 pound pork sausage
6 English muffins, split
   butter for muffins
1 cup apple butter

12 slices American cheese
12 cherry tomatoes
   parsley

Cut pork sausage in 12 even slices or form 12 patties. Brown on both sides in frying pan. While sausage is cooking, lightly toast English muffin halves and spread with butter and then with apple butter. Top each with 1 cheese slice, and place on broiler pan. Broil 3 inches from heat until cheese melts. Arrange sausage patties on cheese. Place a wooden pick topped with a small cherry tomato in center of each; garnish with a sprig of parsley. Serves 12.

Sausage Scramble

1 pound sausage
6 eggs

salt to taste
freshly ground pepper

Brown sausage, breaking up with fork so that sausage is crumbled but not hard. Pour off excess fat. Beat eggs in a bowl and scramble into sausage. Serves 6.

Sausage and Baked Apples

6 *large apples*
1 *cup sausage*

2 *tablespoons brown sugar*

Slice off tops of apples. Scoop out cores and pulp, leaving shells about ¾ inch thick. Chop pulp and combine with sausage and brown sugar. Cook for 15 minutes. Drain. Fill apples with mixture. Bake at 375° until done, approximately 45 minutes. Serves 6.

Sausage Scrapple

2 *pounds sausage*
1 *large can evaporated milk*
3 *cups water*
1½ *cups yellow cornmeal*
   salt

freshly ground pepper
2 *cups crushed corn flakes*
2 *eggs*
4 *tablespoons lard*

Brown sausage and pour off drippings. Combine milk and water. Add 4 cups of liquid to sausage. Reserve remaining liquid. Heat sausage mixture to boiling. Slowly stir in cornmeal and seasonings. Cook 5 minutes, stirring constantly. Pour into a greased loaf pan and chill. Unmold and cut into ½-inch slices. Coat with corn flakes. Combine beaten eggs with remaining liquid. Dip slices in this mixture, then in corn flakes again. Brown both sides in lard. Serves 8 to 10.

Sweets and Sausage

1 *pound cooked link sausage*
1½ *pounds cooked sweet pota-*
   toes, peeled and sliced
8 *slices cooking apple*
1 *can (10½ ounces) condensed*
   consommé

1 *tablespoon cornstarch*
½ *cup sugar*
1 *tablespoon orange juice*
1 *teaspoon grated lemon rind*
½ *cup chopped pecans*

Combine sausage, sweet potatoes and apple slices in a large frying pan. In a saucepan, over low heat, blend consommé, cornstarch, sugar, orange juice and lemon rind until thick. Then add to sausage. Continue to cook over low heat for 20 minutes, spooning glaze over continuously. Add pecans. Serves 4.

CLEOPATRA'S BREAKFAST

"Mark Antony, at one of his breakfasts with Cleopatra, had eight wild boars *roasted whole; and though the Romans do not appear to have been addicted to hunting, wild-boar fights formed part of their gladiatorial shows in the amphitheatre."*

—*from Mrs. Isabella Beeton's* Book of Household Management, *1861.*

EARLIEST CURERS OF HAM

"The salting and smoking of pork to produce ham is of French origin. It was, in fact, the Gauls, great devotees of pig meat and very efficient pig-breeders, who first became renowned for the salting, smoking and curing of the various cuts of pork. . . .

"This, according to reliable documentary evidence, is how the Gauls cured their hams:

"After salting them, they subjected them for two days to the smoke of certain selected woods. Then they rubbed them with oil and vinegar and hung them up, to dry and preserve them."

—*from* Larousse Gastronomique, the Encyclopedia of Food, Wine & Cookery, *by Prosper Montagné, Crown Publishers, Inc., New York, p. 480.*

5

How to
Cure Ham at Home

I DON'T EXPECT that many housewives today would attempt to cure country ham, especially since the smoked and cured hams from Virginia, Kentucky, Tennessee and Georgia are so readily available. But the Back to Mother Earth movement is bringing about a resurgence of pig breeding and a new need to know about home curing methods.

The Talmadge hams and others commercially distributed are cured under the most rigid regulations of the Pure Food and Drug Administration. The method of curing, described in James A. Christian's *Curing Georgia Hams—Country Style,** a booklet put out by the University of Georgia's Cooperative Extension Service, can be applied to on-the-farm curing for family use.

Early in my ham-business experience, I followed steps similar to those set forth in this publication and I can verify the fact that it is not difficult to cure pork if a few basic principles in curing, salt equalization and aging are closely observed.

Briefly, here are some specific instructions, but a thorough study of the subject should be made before you slaughter the pig!

Refrigeration, either by machinery or from our normal weather conditions in the fall and winter, is essential in a ham-curing operation.

The most desirable slaughter weight is 180 to 240 pounds.

Kill hogs only when the weatherman predicts a heavy frost or

* Bulletin 627 can be obtained by writing Cooperative Extension Service, College of Agriculture, University of Georgia, Athens, Georgia.

when the temperature is 32 to 35° F. Souring bacteria multiply rapidly at temperatures above 40°. Meat should be cured *immediately* after slaughtering. (Hogs can be slaughtered on the farm and taken immediately to a processing plant for chilling, and there the carcass can be properly processed and the hams properly cured under refrigeration.)

Do not attempt to cure a ham that shows signs of being bruised; it will spoil during the curing process.

Begin curing as soon as possible after hams are chilled and cut.

A good curing mixture is 8 pounds of salt, 3 pounds of sugar and 3 ounces of saltpeter. Apply the mix at the rate of 1¼ ounces per pound of meat. Use ⅓ the mixture on the first day, ⅓ on the 3rd day, and the last ⅓ on the 10th day. Rub it in thoroughly each time.

Weigh the ham to get the exact amount of cure to use. Good salt penetration requires 7 days per inch of thickness. Bacon requires from 14 to 16 days. Add another day to the curing schedule for each day the weather is below freezing.

After this period, wash the outside coating of salt off and leave the meat at a temperature below 40° for another 20 to 25 days for salt equalization. Then smoke the meat, if desired. Don't allow the temperature in the smokehouse to exceed 100°. Use hickory, oak or apple wood as fuel. The smokehouse should be sealed and ventilated with fans, or completely screened for natural ventilation.

Smoke hams until they are amber or mahogany in color (usually about 2 days) .

Mountain families have successfully cured and smoked hams for years without reading up on the subject, but I hope any novice farmer today who hasn't learned the method from his forefathers will seek expert advice before the first frost.

Since almost every part of the pig can in some way be cured, cooked, canned or pickled, a serious cook may want to refer to the "Pig'lossary" and the recipes in the next chapter.

6

Pig'lossary
with Recipes for Everything
from Pigs' Ears to Pigs' Tails

CHITTERLINGS (better known as Chitlins) Small intestines of the pig

CRACKLINGS (Cracklin's) Crisp bits left when pork fat has been rendered; often added to corn bread to make Cracklin' Bread

HEADCHEESE Meat from pigs' heads, tongues, hearts and other pieces, boiled and ground, seasoned and chilled; usually eaten cold as an appetizer

HOG A pig, usually one weighing over 120 pounds

HOG MAW Tripe

HOPPIN' JOHN Black-eyed peas mixed with rice and cooked with a ham butt

JOWLS Hog jaw

KNUCKLES (also called Pork Hocks) The ankle bone just above the cloven hoof

LIGHTS Lungs of pigs

LIVER SAUSAGE Ground meat consisting of cooked pig's head, liver, tongue, heart and other pieces

PANHAS A mush consisting of soup remaining from boiling pig parts combined with cornmeal

PICKLED PIGS' FEET Cleaned pigs' feet, pickled

PIG A young domesticated hog

PORK HOCKS Pigs' knuckles

PORK TAILS Tasty pork from pigs' tails, often cooked with greens

RED-EYE GRAVY Juices and liquid from skillet in which slices of country ham have been cooked

SCRAPPLE Cooked and ground pork, thickened with cornmeal and flour, chilled, sliced and fried quickly. Also called "Ponhaws" by the Pennsylvania Dutch

SOUSE Pressed pork (meat jellied from pigs' tails, feet, knuckles or head) served as appetizer for a luncheon or dinner

SWEETBREADS Thymus of an animal

TOM THUMBS Cooked chitlins cut into short lengths, usually coated with flour or cornmeal and fried

TRIPE (also called Hog Maw) Inner lining of a pig's stomach (a calf's stomach lining is also called Tripe)

TROTTERS British name for pigs' feet

PIG'LOSSARY RECIPES

Extra-Fancy Chitlins
Pepper Stock for Pork
City-Style Cracklin's
Pigs' Knuckles and Sauerkraut
Souse
Tongue with Raisin-Cranberry
    Sauce
Sweetbreads with Spinach

Scrapple
Headcheese
Liver Sausage
Panhas
Pig's Liver and Lights
Pigs' Ears
Pigs' Tails
Pickled Pigs' Feet

Extra-Fancy Chitlins

Chitlins, found cooked or uncooked in most supermarkets today, are already cleaned and packaged frozen in 5- to 10-pound packages. (Cooked chitlins are expensive, but they can be used immediately, since they are already in a sauce.)

5 pounds chitlins (raw, frozen)

Soak in cold water to thaw. Turn inside out to pick and cook. Pick off any excess fat with your fingers. Simmer in Pepper Stock, below.

To fry: drain chitlins from stock. Cut into short lengths, pepper heavily and coat with cornmeal. Drop them in hot fat to brown and crisp. Drain well.

Some say these are good enough to serve with champagne.

Pepper Stock for Pork

1 quart water	*½ teaspoon garlic powder*
1 teaspoon salt	*1 bay leaf*
1 large onion, quartered	*¼ cup vinegar (white or cider)*
¼ teaspoon hot red pepper	*2 whole cloves*

Combine all ingredients. Bring liquid to a boil and add chitlins. Simmer about 2½ hours. (Pigs' feet, pigs' tails, pigs' knuckles and tripe can all be cooked in this stock.)

City-Style Cracklin's

Few stores, particularly in Washington, have cracklin's, but I like to serve cracklin' bread with fresh vegetables, so I've learned to make my own. Here's my city-style cracklin's:

Trim fat off a ham or pork roast, or purchase 1 pound of "fatback." Cut into small pieces, put pieces in pot with ½ cup water, stir and cook until water is gone and the small pieces of fat are crisp and brown.

Pigs' Knuckles and Sauerkraut

Wash and scrape pigs' knuckles and simmer in water, covered, for 2 hours. Add sauerkraut to broth in quantity desired and cook until meat is very tender and broth is almost evaporated. Season to taste with salt, pepper and celery seed or caraway seed.

Souse

*Even though the cooking of pigs' feet or knuckles may be
a new experience for you, you should try making Souse. It is
a delicacy, delicious served cold in the summer.*

4 pigs' knuckles, feet, jowls and/   ½ cup minced parsley
   or other pork parts   salt and pepper to taste
grated fresh onion (about
   2 tablespoons)

Cook pork trimmings in Pepper Stock (p. 126). When meat is tender,
remove from bone, strain stock, and refrigerate both. Remove fat from
stock and cut meat into small pieces. Reduce stock to 3 cups, add meat,
onion and parsley. Season to taste. Mold into loaf pan and pour some
of the stock over meat. Cover with waxed paper and put a weight on
top to press meat. It will be a firm loaf after refrigeration. To be fancy,
place the loaf on a bed of spinach leaves and surround it with bite-
sized raw vegetables before serving. Serves 8.

Tongue with Raisin-Cranberry Sauce

  1 pork tongue   *1½ cups stock*
  3 tablespoons butter   *2 tablespoons seedless raisins*
1½ teaspoons minced onion   *⅓ cup cranberry sauce*
  3 tablespoons flour   *1 bay leaf, crumbled*

Place tongue in covered kettle with boiling water to cover and simmer
3 hours. Remove from heat and let tongue stand in liquid until cool.
Remove skin and fat from tongue and cut into slices about ⅜ inch
thick. In a heavy skillet, melt the butter, add the onion and cook until
clear; add flour and blend thoroughly. Add the stock and cook until
thickened, stirring frequently. Place sliced tongue in the pan with
gravy, add raisins, cranberry sauce and bay leaf. Simmer, covered, for
30 minutes. Serves 6.

Sweetbreads with Spinach

6 *pair sweetbreads*	2 *tablespoons sherry*
2 *tablespoons flour*	½ *teaspoon tomato paste*
1 *beaten egg*	1 *teaspoon potato starch*
½ *cup bread crumbs*	¾ *cup stock*
2 *tablespoons butter*	

Place sweetbreads in pan, cover with cold water and bring to a boil. Drain and soak in a little cold water to cool. Carefully remove skin and sinews. Cut in half lengthwise and dust lightly with flour, then dip in beaten egg and roll in bread crumbs. Fry very quickly on each side in hot butter. Pour sherry over them. Cover and cook very slowly for 10 minutes, turn and cook another 10 minutes. Remove and add to pan the tomato paste, the potato starch and the stock. Prepare **Spinach,** below.

SPINACH

2 *pounds spinach*	*freshly ground pepper*
2 *tablespoons bacon drippings*	½ *pint sour cream*
salt	

Wash spinach well. Drain and place in pan with bacon drippings, salt and pepper to taste. Cover. Cook briskly 8 minutes. Drain well and chop in bowl. Mix in the sour cream. Arrange on bottom of serving dish. Place the sweetbreads on top and pour the sauce over all. Serves 6 to 8.

Scrapple

Scrapple is a breakfast dish originated by the Pennsylvania Dutch around 1683, made of cooked pork and broth thickened with cornmeal, flour, and sometimes "shorts" (bran mixed with coarse meal or flour).

Cook the pig's head, heart and trimmings as for Headcheese (p. 129), or until the bones can be removed. Remove bones and grind meat. Return all ground meat to the strained broth and bring to a boil. The cereal mixture to be added may vary widely. A mixture consisting of 7 parts cornmeal to 3 parts white or buckwheat flour or one of 7 parts cornmeal to 2 parts "shorts" and 1 part buckwheat flour is acceptable. In adding the cereal mixture, moisten it with some of the cooled broth so that it may be added to the hot broth without forming lumps. Boil for about 30 minutes; stir constantly to prevent sticking. Add the seasoning shortly before the cooking is finished and stir in well. (Use salt, black pepper, marjoram, sage, nutmeg, mace, ground onions, red pepper.) Pour hot scrapple into small, shallow pans and chill as promptly as possible. Then unmold, slice and fry quickly. This is sometimes referred to as Philadelphia Scrapple.

Headcheese

Cook pigs' heads, tongues, hearts and other pieces. Make deep cuts in thick pieces of meat, cover with water and simmer until the meat is well done and slips easily from the bones. Remove bones from bony pieces after cooking. Grind boned meat with the boneless pieces (such as the heart). Return this mixture to the broth and bring to a boil. This reheating mixes the headcheese and makes it thicker. Add seasoning. Use salt, black pepper, red pepper, ground cloves, coriander (if desired) and sweet marjoram, and let all simmer 30 minutes. Pour into loaf pans and chill. It will slice without difficulty. Store in refrigerator. Headcheese is usually eaten cold, often served with vinegar.

Liver Sausage

Cook heads, tongues, hearts and other pieces as for Headcheese (above) but for a shorter period. Remove from heat when meat can be boned; bone as necessary. Then *scald the livers.* (If you cut them deeply with a knife, they will be sufficiently scalded in about 10 minutes.) Grind all cooked meat moderately fine. Add only enough liquid from cooked meat to make the mixture soft but not sloppy. Season with salt, pepper, herbs and spices to taste and mix thoroughly. Simmer 30 minutes. Stuff into beef casings or loaf pan or mold. Chill.

Panhas

Use the soup remaining after making headcheese or liver sausage to make a kind of cornmeal mush called Panhas. Strain out all bones, bring the soup to a boil, and add the meal slowly. Three or 4 parts of soup to 1 part meal, by volume, is a good proportion. Season to taste with the seasonings given for Headcheese (p. 129). Cook the meal 30 to 45 minutes and pour it into shallow pans to cool. Slice and serve like scrapple.*

Pig's Liver and Lights

I don't know how this recipe came to our kitchen, but I suspect from the way in which it is written that it was copied out of an old English cookbook. It is referred to as "a Savoury and Economical Dish."

INGREDIENTS: The liver and lights of a pig, 6 or 7 slices of bacon, potatoes, 1 bunch of parsley, 2 onions, 2 sage-leaves, pepper and salt to taste, a little broth or water.

INSTRUCTIONS: Slice the liver and lights and wash these clean; parboil the potatoes; mince the parsley and sage, and chop the onion. Put meat, potatoes and bacon into a deep dish, in alternate layers, with a sprinkling of the herbs, seasoning with salt and pepper; pour on a little water or broth, and bake in a moderately heated oven for 2 hours. Serves 6 or 7.

Pigs' Ears

You can go down to the Atlanta Municipal Market today where all the farmers bring their fresh produce and find a luncheon stand sell-

---

* Recipes for Headcheese, Liver Sausage, Panhas, Souse and Scrapple are from "Slaughtering, Cutting & Processing Pork on the Farm," Farmers' Bulletin #2138, U.S. Department of Agriculture.

ing pigs' ear sandwiches. I asked the man behind the stand how he cooked them:

"Just boil 'em in salt water with a little vinegar added until you can stick a fork in 'em," he said. He admitted that he used to sell fifteen or twenty a day, but now that they cost as much as a good bowl of Brunswick stew, he sells only five or six a day.

Pigs' Tails

The demand for pigs' tails might be greater if the general public knew how tender they can be. Just boil them (1 to a serving) in well-seasoned water (use the Pepper Stock, p. 126). When tender, remove from stock and, if desired, brown in oven before serving.

Pickled Pigs' Feet

Pickled pigs' feet are, of course, available in most markets. I know, because I distribute them through Betty Talmadge & Associates. You can also buy fresh, cleaned pigs' feet from meat markets. Be sure to wash them thoroughly.

To PICKLE: Place clean, chilled feet in brine for 15 days to 3 weeks. Make the brine by dissolving 1 pound salt, ¼ pound sugar, and ¼ ounce saltpeter in 9 cups of water. Weight the feet to keep them from floating above the solution. Keep pork cold (36° to 40° F., if possible) throughout curing period.

To COOK: Simmer cured feet slowly until they are tender. Thoroughly chill the cured, cooked feet and pack them in cold, moderately strong vinegar, to which you can add spices such as bay leaves or allspice. Use the feet at once, or keep them in the vinegar for about 3 weeks.

PROVERBIAL PIG PHRASES

As independent as a hog on ice . . .
To go the whole hog . . .
To buy a pig in a poke . . .
As fat as a pig . . .
Dead as a stuck pig . . .
As good-natured as a suckling pig . . .
As happy as a pig in paradise . . .
In a pig's eye . . .
Frisking about like pigs in clover . . .
Screamin' like a stuck pig . . .
Stiffened out like a frozen pig . . .
In less time than a pig's whistle . . .
Eatin' high on the hog . . .
Can't make a silk purse out of a sow's ear . . .
Fat as a hog . . .
As the old hog squeals, the young ones learn . . .
Root, hog, or die . . .
To know no more than a hog does about a holiday . . .
Sleep like a hog . . .
Hog-tied . . .
In hog heaven . . .

PART III

Poultry in the Pot

HERMAN AND I FOUND OUR WAY into the meat-processing industry only after having tried and failed miserably in several other ventures. Let the following be a lesson to any who might decide to take up farming for fun.

We were told that wild turkeys would be a fine addition to the farm. So we purchased a half dozen or so and turned them loose. They were supposed to scatter to the fields and forests, grow and multiply. Instead, they all settled down on the front porch of our farmhouse. What a mess! After a few weeks, we gave up. I don't know whether you can tame a real wild turkey, but I know for sure you can't make a tame turkey wild.

Another time I decided to have a garlic farm. I even hired an Oriental gardener to help me. But he got so interested in watching the vegetables grow to outlandish sizes that the garlic crop failed and our overgrown vegetables couldn't be marketed.

Next we tried raising minks. We have a lake near the farm, and that seemed like a perfect place for a mink ranch. We were sure we would realize a handsome income by buying a few minks, raising them and selling the pelts at a nice figure. I even had visions of owning a homegrown mink coat.

On paper, I figured each female mink would produce four little ones at suitable intervals and the stock would be quadrupled annually. I discovered that minks can't work arithmetic.

Our most unsuccessful business venture: raising mink.

But they were cute little critters!

We invested in twenty minks, sent from Minnesota, and the reproduction rate wasn't as high as we expected. It just wasn't a good year for mink. As I recall, that was the year that Washington hummed with mink-coat scandals, so maybe they felt depressed or maybe they didn't like the weather—minks need a cooler climate than Georgia mostly has. In any case, the death rate climbed. Or perhaps they had an inadequate diet, because I discovered that those little critters were actually eating each other up! At one time or another, we were equally financially unsuccessful at raising Shetland ponies, hogs, chickens and cattle. I finally made a firm resolution: Never get into a business that involves anything that eats or has to be fertilized.

So Herman decided to plant most of the acreage in pine trees. They take care of themselves, fed and watered by nature. And we both agreed not to raise our own pigs, but rather to put to use an old family recipe for the aging and curing of ham. Processed country hams were a natural product for us to bring to the public.

One of my friends, the vice-president of a large supermarket chain, told me that I had more courage than sense when I went into the ham business. I replied that Mr. H. L. Hunt, the oil billionaire, once said he was sure glad he had never been hampered in *his* business by an *education!*

I don't really feel that way, of course. Even though I didn't finish college before I married, I have been back to take courses that have helped me gain confidence in making decisions in business.

The first course I took in bookkeeping was at the Benjamin Franklin School of Accounting in Washington, D.C. I was pretty proud of myself when I called on our accountant in Georgia after finishing that course and made a few recommendations. Bill Stribling, head of the accounting firm, listened patiently to my suggestions and then said, "Betty, no one is more trying than a half-educated woman!"

But he had to admit later that my little bit of knowledge had saved several thousand dollars in taxable income.

Ten years later, I decided to get the *other half* of that education Mr. Stribling mentioned. I still haven't quite made the finish line, but I'm a long way from the days when I didn't know a debit from a credit!

I enrolled in business school at American University. I passed my courses with A's and B's—which I never could have done in my earlier college days—and then decided to launch another business called "Betty Talmadge & Associates."

We are meat sales representatives. I would describe the business as a specialized meat service organization. My partner is a man. We have two women working for us and, as of this date, five accounts. We market products such as chickens and turkeys, pickled pigs' feet (from Brooklyn, New York, of all places!), Talmadge country-cured hams, Danish canned hams, crabs and a full line of other meats. Essentially, we get the buyer and seller together. Instead of having a fleet of salesmen for five companies, we represent them all when we go to the stores. The stores deal only with one company for a number of different products. It works to advantage for everyone, including Betty Talmadge & Associates. Some experts told me we would not be in the black for three years, but we made it in four months!

I retained an interest in Talmadge Hams when we joined forces with the Cagles, who had for years been in the chicken industry. Cagle's, Inc., now processes our hams along with various poultry products.

To my mind, Southern fried chicken—if it is fried in lard at just the right temperature—is hard to beat. The flavor of chicken will stand alone when it is fried, broiled or baked. But it often is not considered "gourmet" unless you add the subtle flavors of fruit, spices or wine.

If you are a calorie counter—and I am—chicken can help you out. It is high in protein, vitamin A, niacin and calcium and low in calories and saturated fats. Chicken is also easy to digest, great for youngsters and older people or those who need a bland ulcer diet or require soft foods.

I'm sure I couldn't entertain without grits, ham and chicken. They all complement each other. Put them together with a salad and almost any vegetable, and your menu is complete.

At the Talmadge farm, my favorite plates set for luncheon are English earthenware (B & L Ltd.) and contain this verse:

Let the wealthy and great
Roll in splendor and state
I envy them not, I declare it
I eat my own lamb
My own chickens and ham
I share my own fleece and I wear it
I have lawns, I have bowers
I have fruits, I have flowers
The lark is my morning alarmer
So jolly boys now here's God speed the plow
Long life and success to the Farmer

1

A Chicken
Cookout

I'VE COLLECTED some chicken recipes with a flair, but my own favorite is the one I use when we have a chicken cookout.

CHICKEN COOKOUT

Southern Barbecued Chicken
Country Fried Ham with Red-eye Gravy
Spinach Salad (p. 72)
'Cile's Corn Bread (p. 38)
Fresh Corn Casserole (p. 46)
Ruby's Red Candied Apples
Boiled Custard (p. 202), Ice Cream

Using the same basic menu, I often serve crisp fried chicken, or fried ham slices topped with chicken-breast fillets and slices of country sausage, instead of the barbecued chicken.

Southern Barbecued Chicken

I like to use the Country Barbecue Sauce (p. 40) for this recipe, particularly because it can be used to barbecue chicken on a grill, or, if you are in a hurry, as I often am, you can just pour it over the chicken and bake it uncovered at 350° F. for 1 hour. The sauce can be made ahead of time; it keeps for weeks in a jar in the refrigerator. Fresh ginger is the secret of its flavor.

ON THE GRILL: Place chicken halves which have been sprinkled with salt and pepper and rubbed with oil on the hot grill. Brush on the Country Barbecue Sauce and cook for 10 minutes. Turn and baste the other side. Turn and baste every 10 minutes until the chickens are done.

IN THE OVEN: Place the chicken halves or parts skin side up in a shallow baking pan. Pour sauce generously over the chicken and place in oven. Bake for 1 hour without turning or basting.

Country Fried Ham with Red-eye Gravy

You can now purchase in many stores country-cured ham that is already sliced and packaged. But for a party it would be more economical to buy a whole country-cured ham and have as much as you need sliced ¼ inch thick. Your friendly butcher will do this for you. Trim off skin, leaving as much fat as possible. Soak the ham slices for 15 minutes in warm water (or 30 minutes in one cup buttermilk or sweet milk in which 3 tablespoons of brown sugar have been dissolved). Drain the ham, place in a preheated skillet and brown each side of the ham at medium heat. To make Red-eye Gravy, remove the ham from the pan, add a little water to the drippings and simmer. (Some add coffee instead of water.) Serve piping hot.

Leftover country-cured ham has many uses. For hors d'oeuvres, fasten shaved baked ham around pieces of fruit with wooden picks; or make tiny open-face sliced baked ham canapés on thin rye bread; or put fried ham in tiny hot biscuits; or make small sandwiches with melted cheese and shaved baked ham.

Ruby's Red Candied Apples

My friend Ruby Wimberly told me how to do these colorful candied apples, so I named them for her.

3 cups sugar
2 cups boiling water
1- ounce package of cinnamon
    hearts ("red hots," as the
    children call them)

12 apples, cored and peeled

Cook sugar and water 15 minutes. Add package of cinnamon hearts and bring to a very hard boil. Drop in apples, cored and peeled. With a slotted spoon roll them over and over slowly (do not pick them up). After the apples are heated through, watch carefully to see that they do not burn. Remove immediately. Refrigerate. It is best to cook them a day ahead.

Mrs. Harriet Chester, an ex-slave from Tennessee, described this method as "the best way to cook chicken":

"When we roasted a chicken, we got it all nice and clean, stuffed him with dressing, greased him all over good, put a cabbage leaf on the floor of the fireplace, put the chicken on the cabbage leaf, then covered him good with another cabbage leaf, and put hot coals all over and around him to roast."

—*from* Roll, Jordan, Roll, *Eugene D. Genovese, Vintage Books, Random House, New York, 1972, p. 547.*

2

Other
Poultry Recipes

To TELL THE TRUTH, I sort of backed into the chicken business. Around the time I merged my ham business with Cagle's poultry business, they brought out a new product which has turned me into an international entrepreneur!

The product is chicken wieners.

I had learned that the price of meat in Japan was sky-high, so I decided the Japanese ought to try Cagle's better-tasting, cheaper-to-produce chicken variety wiener. Why not have my new firm, Betty Talmadge & Associates, market them in Japan?

So off to Japan I went, armed with a batch of wieners. I was amazed to learn that most important decisions over there are made by committees. That is not often the case in this country. I was reminded of the time Lady Bird Johnson and I were riding through an American city during her beautification campaign when she quietly pointed out a hodgepodge garden area and said, "That looks like it was planted by a committee!"

I presented my proposal to market chicken wieners in Japan, and a "committee" agreed to come to Lovejoy to discuss the matter further with me.

A month later, a representative "committee" came to the farm to meet with our people. I served the ten men present a luncheon that I'm sure they'll never forget.

We had every variety of chicken wiener: wieners-in-a-blanket (wrapped in crescent rolls); corn dogs; wieners and barbecue sauce; wieners boiled and grilled. I also exposed them to grits, but I don't believe I won them over to that product.

*I launched my new import-
export business in Japan.*

*We're still wondering
whose bare feet are show-
ing under the table!*

I could see they were enthusiastic about the possibility of intro-
ducing chicken wieners to Japan. The Japanese are great baseball
lovers, and what's better during a game than a hot dog with a
Coca-Cola? Marketing them together seemed a natural.

By the end of lunch, we had agreed to give it a try. They ordered
15 metric tons! Washington, D.C., columnist Betty Beale got wind
of the agreement, declared me the "Wienies Winner" and suggested jokingly that they erect a statue to me in Japan. I told her
I'd be happy to settle for another order.

That venture launched my international entrepreneurship.

I decided to explore the market for all the Talmadge products—
not just chicken wieners. So several months later I returned to
Japan, this time with friends who had business experience there—

141

John and Elena Amos. They helped me through the formalities of announcing my new venture with Linder International. I wanted to let the Japanese dignitaries know how much I appreciated their cooperation, so when I spoke at a dinner I compared the similarities between the Japanese traditional courtesies and our "Southern hospitality." Then I let them know my recipe for a successful business undertaking. It must have these ingredients:

1. It must be difficult—or everybody else would be in the business.

2. It must be profitable—to justify the efforts.

3. *Above all,* it must be fun.

I even managed to say a word or two in Japanese, with a Southern accent, of course. I'm sure they couldn't understand what I said, but they liked my attempt to speak their language.

That evening we had the best catfish I ever tasted, and I've tasted a lot. Back in my childhood we had as much catfish, caught fresh in nearby ponds, as ham. They told me Japan imports catfish from the United States, mostly from Georgia and other Southern states, so I thought I would like to have the recipe. Even though this is a country ham and chicken cookbook, I have to include the recipe they so graciously shared with me as I departed.

TOKYO MARUICHI SHOJI CO., LTD.
CATFISH COOKING

1) MATERIALS
SOY SAUCE—enough volume that fish can be soaked into.
RED WINE—a little.
RAW GINGER—to mix with sherry after ground and squeezed moisture, a little.
SUGAR—a bit more.
SALT—a little.
SEASONING—a little.
CHOPPED ONION—a little.

2) ALL OF THE ABOVE TO MIX TOGETHER AND TO SOAK FISH INTO FOR A HALF DAY.

3) ROAST FISH IN AN OVEN.

POULTRY RECIPES

Actually, poultry is even more versatile than ham. A dash of spice, a pinch of herbs, a wine sauce—whatever you wish to pull from the cupboard—creates a new chicken recipe. You can be creative with poultry.

Baked Chicken
Chicken Stew
Dumplings for Chicken Stew
Stewed Chicken with Tomatoes
Rotisseried Chicken
Smothered Chicken
Chicken on Biscuits
Braised Chicken with Vegetables
Chicken for Company
Chicken and Bean Casserole
Daisy Bonner's Country Captain
Carter Family Chicken Supreme
Carter Family Chicken and Rice
   Casserole

Honeyed Chicken
Cold Chicken Loaf
Hot Chicken Salad
Chicken Pie
Pressed Chicken
Super Chicken
Stuffed Doves
Braised Quail
Creamed Ham and Chicken
Corn Bread Stuffing for Turkey or
   Chicken

Baked Chicken

Chickens are less expensive if you buy them whole. They are easy to disjoint with a sharp, heavy knife or poultry shears, and easy to bake.

Clean and disjoint 2 young chickens. Salt, pepper, dip in flour, beaten egg and then in soft bread crumbs. Place in a well-greased roaster or casserole and bake, uncovered, for 30 minutes in a 400° F. oven, basting at least once with ⅓ cup melted butter or margarine. When tender, place chicken on platter and pour over it 2 cups of Basic Cream Sauce (p. 26) to which ¼ cup chopped parsley has been added. Serves 6 to 8.

Chicken Stew

1 large stewing hen (4 or 5
    pounds)
2 stalks celery, chopped
2 carrots, diced
2 onions, chopped

1 teaspoon Tabasco sauce
    salt and pepper to taste
6 medium-size potatoes, peeled
    and parboiled
1 cup Basic Cream Sauce

Quarter chicken and place it in a deep pot with enough water to cover. Add celery, carrots, onions and seasonings, and simmer until chicken is tender. Remove chicken from broth and bone it. Add potatoes to broth and simmer until potatoes are done. Add boned chicken to reheat. To thicken, add 1 cup Basic Cream Sauce (p. 26, but made with broth from chicken stew). Serves 6.

    Variation: Omit potatoes and cream sauce and add Dumplings, below.

DUMPLINGS
2 cups flour
4 teaspoons baking powder

1 teaspoon salt
1 cup milk

Sift together dry ingredients and gradually add milk to make dough. Drop by spoonfuls into simmering stew. Cover and boil rapidly for 10 minutes.

Stewed Chicken with Tomatoes

2 fryers, cut up
8 cups water
4 cups chopped fresh (or
    canned) tomatoes
1 clove garlic
    salt and pepper to taste

½ cup brown or white rice,
    uncooked
6 large carrots, chopped
6 white onions (or leeks),
    quartered

Simmer chicken in water with tomatoes, garlic, salt and pepper. When chicken is just tender, remove from broth; bone. Simmer rice, carrots and onions in broth for 15 minutes; add chicken pieces and simmer another 15 minutes. Serves 8.

Rotisseried Chicken

I came to this recipe when I first started trying to cut calories. I love chicken and I wanted to keep the good natural flavor.

Take 1 whole fryer, weighing 2½ to 3½ pounds and, if there is time, marinate it in lemon juice overnight. If this is not convenient, cover it with Lemon Pepper seasoning, inside and out. Tie wings and legs with string, put it on an oven or grill rotisserie skewer and cook about 45 minutes to 1 hour. Serves 4.

Smothered Chicken

1 large fryer cut in pieces
lard or cooking oil
salt and pepper to taste

2 cups Basic Cream Sauce
(p. 26)

On top of stove, brown chicken pieces quickly in hot deep fat. Remove; drain thoroughly. Salt and pepper to taste. Place pieces in a heavy iron Dutch oven or a casserole and cover with Basic Cream Sauce. Simmer for 1 hour. Place in a slow oven (275° F.) to cook for 1 hour. Serve with rice or cheese grits. Serves 4.

Chicken on Biscuits

2 tablespoons finely chopped
  onion
¼ cup chopped green pepper
1 cup green peas
1 cup water
⅔ cup flour
1 cup cold milk
2 cups chicken broth

2 teaspoons salt
freshly ground black pepper
½ teaspoon poultry seasoning
2 cups diced cooked chicken
1 tablespoon pimiento
1 4-ounce can mushrooms
  (stems and pieces)

Simmer onion, green pepper and green peas in water in a covered pan for 5 minutes. Drain; save the liquid. Combine flour and milk. Over low heat, slowly stir vegetable cooking liquid, broth, and seasonings into flour mixture. Bring to a boil, stirring constantly. Cook for 1 minute. Add chicken, cooked vegetables, pimiento and mushrooms. Heat thoroughly and serve on biscuits. Serves 6.

Braised Chicken with Vegetables

½ *cup flour*
  1 teaspoon salt
    freshly ground black pepper
  3- pound chicken cut into pieces
  3 tablespoons oil
¾ *cup hot water*

½ *teaspoon salt*
¾ *cup chopped green pepper*
  3 cups sliced celery
1½ *cups sliced carrots*
¾ *cup finely chopped onion*

Combine flour, salt and pepper; coat chicken pieces with mixture. Brown chicken in hot fat in large frying pan. Drain excess fat from pan. Add water and salt. Cover tightly and simmer 45 minutes. Add vegetables and cook 30 minutes longer. Serves 6.

Chicken for Company

2 tablespoons oil
2 tablespoons butter
6 large chicken breasts (boned and rolled)
1 can cream of chicken soup
1 cup light cream

½ *cup sherry*
  1 can (4 or 6 ounces) sliced mushrooms, drained
    pineapple tidbits
    seedless grapes

Heat oil and butter in baking dish. Roll chicken breasts in fat and bake for 1 hour at 350° F. Heat soup, cream and sherry in saucepan. Stir in mushrooms. Remove baking dish from oven. Pour off excess fat. Spoon soup mixture over chicken. Cover baking dish with aluminum foil. Bake an additional 15 to 20 minutes. Garnish with pineapple tidbits and grapes. Serves 6.

Chicken and Bean Casserole

3½ *cups of cooked fresh or frozen*
 French-style string beans
3 *whole chicken breasts, boiled,*
 skinned, boned and halved
2 *cans condensed cream of*
 chicken soup

1 *cup mayonnaise*
1 *teaspoon lemon juice*
½ *cup grated sharp cheese*
½ *cup buttered bread crumbs*

Drain beans and arrange in buttered baking dish. Place chicken breasts on top of beans. Combine soup, mayonnaise and lemon juice. Pour over chicken. Sprinkle with cheese and top with buttered crumbs. Bake at 350° F. for 30 minutes. Serves 6.

Daisy Bonner's Country Captain

Daisy Bonner cooked for President Franklin D. Roosevelt at his home at Warm Springs, Georgia. With Country Captain she usually served baked grapefruit, French beans, plain salad, rolls, chocolate soufflé and coffee.

1 *hen or 2 fryers*
2 *or 3 green peppers, chopped*
2 *onions, chopped*
1 *can (16 ounces) tomatoes*
1 *can (4 to 6 ounces)*
 mushrooms
¼ *cup almonds or other nuts for*
 sauce
1 *pod garlic, crushed*

¼ *cup raisins for sauce*
1 *teaspoon thyme*
 salt and pepper to taste
1 *teaspoon curry powder (or*
 more to taste)
2 *cups rice, cooked until dry*
¼ *cup raisins for garnish*
¼ *cup almonds or other nuts for*
 garnish

Boil chicken until just done. Bone. Make sauce with the green peppers, onions, tomatoes, mushrooms, ¼ cup almonds, garlic, ¼ cup raisins, thyme, salt, pepper, and curry powder. Add chicken. Let simmer on top of stove or in the oven for 1 hour. Serve over rice. Garnish with mixture of raisins and nuts. Serves 6 to 8.

Carter Family
Chicken Supreme

4 boned whole chicken breasts,
    halved
cardamom
chervil
salt and pepper
1 egg

1/4 cup milk
bread crumbs
butter or margarine
2 ounces brandy
4 tablespoons Burgundy
1 pint chicken stock

Season chicken breasts with cardamom, chervil, salt and pepper. Dip into egg and milk, beaten together, then dip into fine bread crumbs. Brown on both sides in butter or margarine until tender. Place chicken in baking dish. Pour the brandy, Burgundy and chicken stock over the chicken. Bake in moderate oven (350° F.) until tender. Serves 4 to 8.

Carter Family
Chicken and Rice Casserole

1 chicken cut into serving pieces
1/2 stick butter
1 4-ounce can mushrooms,
    drained (save liquid)

4 large onions, sliced into rings
2 chicken bouillon cubes
1 cup uncooked rice (do not use
    quick-cooking rice)

Melt butter in casserole. Layer chicken pieces in casserole with onions and mushrooms. Cook, covered, for 1 hour at 350° F. Add enough boiling water to mushroom liquid to make 4½ cups of broth. Dissolve chicken bouillon cubes in broth. Pour into casserole. Add rice. Cook, covered, for 1 hour more. Serves 4.

Honeyed Chicken

1/2 cup peanut oil
2 eggs

2 tablespoons water
2½-pound chicken

1 cup flour
1 teaspoon salt
freshly ground pepper

1 cup hot water
¼ cup honey
1 cup orange juice

Heat oil in skillet. Beat eggs with 2 tablespoons water. Dip chicken pieces in egg mixture, then roll in flour to which salt and pepper have been added. Brown in hot oil. Place chicken in casserole dish. Mix the 1 cup hot water, honey and orange juice; pour over chicken. Bake at 325° F. for 1 hour. Serves 4.

Cold Chicken Loaf

1 package lemon gelatin
2 cups hot chicken stock or
  bouillon
1 cup diced cooked chicken
½ cup celery, chopped
¼ cup chopped green olives
¼ cup chopped green peppers

2 tablespoons diced pimiento
2 tablespoons vinegar
1 teaspoon grated onion
¼ teaspoon salt
½ teaspoon pepper
dash Worcestershire sauce

Pour gelatin into hot stock and stir until dissolved; chill until slightly thickened. Combine other ingredients and fold into gelatin and turn into mold. Chill, unmold and slice. Serves 6 to 8.

Hot Chicken Salad

2 cups diced cooked chicken
½ teaspoon grated onion
2 cups chopped celery
1 cup mayonnaise

2 teaspoons lemon juice
grated Parmesan cheese
1 cup crumbled potato chips
olives

Combine chicken, onion, celery, mayonnaise and lemon juice in baking dish. Cover. Bake at 450° F. for 25 minutes. Top with cheese and potato chips, garnish with sliced olives and bake uncovered for an additional 10 minutes until cheese melts. Serves 4.

Chicken Pie

1 4-pound chicken	*¼ cup flour*
1 cup diced carrots	*1 quart chicken stock*
1 cup green peas	*½ tablespoon salt*
¼ cup chicken fat	*freshly ground pepper*

Boil chicken until tender. Strip meat from the bones. Cut into small pieces. Place layers of chicken and vegetables in individual casseroles. Cover with sauce made with chicken fat, flour and chicken stock and seasoned with salt and pepper. Cover with pie pastry or a biscuit mix rolled thin. Bake at 400° F. for 30 minutes. Serves 6.

Pressed Chicken

1 large hen or 2 small chickens	*1 cup mayonnaise*
1 large onion	*2 cups diced celery*
1 teaspoon salt	*4 hard-boiled eggs, chopped*
½ teaspoon paprika	*5 tablespoons India relish (or*
¼ teaspoon pepper	*chopped olives)*
1 quart chicken broth	*1½ tablespoons lemon juice*
3 tablespoons plain gelatin soaked in ½ cup cold water	*1 cup chopped toasted almonds*

Cook chicken with onion, salt, paprika and pepper until tender. Bone and dice meat. Reserve at least 1 quart of broth. Strain broth and add gelatin. When gelatin is dissolved, combine with all other ingredients. Mix well. Jell in mold or loaf pan. Serves at least 12.

Super Chicken

4 whole chicken breasts, halved and boned	*12 ounces medium noodles*
4 slices boiled ham, cut in half	*2 teaspoons salt*
3¼ cups water	*1 pint sour cream*
	2 tablespoons flour

1 small jar sliced pimiento   *1 teaspoon salt*
¼ cup finely chopped parsley   *1 cup mushrooms, sautéed*

Place a piece of ham in center of each half breast. Wrap chicken around ham and secure with toothpicks. Arrange chicken, skin sides down, in a heated skillet. Pour ¼ cup water over chicken. Cook, covered, for 30 minutes. Take chicken out of frying pan; remove toothpicks. Keep chicken warm. Lower heat. Add 3 cups of water, noodles, salt to skillet. Cook, covered, for 20 minutes. Combine sour cream, flour, pimiento, parsley and 1 teaspoon salt. Add sautéed mushrooms. Set aside ½ cup sour-cream mixture. Stir remaining sour-cream mixture into noodles. Arrange chicken, skin sides up, on top of noodles. Spoon on reserved sour cream. Simmer, covered, for 10 minutes. Serves 8.

Stuffed Doves

6 doves   *½ stick butter*
  salt   *6 strips bacon*
  freshly ground pepper   *½ cup red wine*
6 chicken livers

Clean and wash doves; salt and pepper. Salt and pepper chicken livers. Place a chicken liver with a pat of butter in cavity of each dove. Tie dove legs together, wrap bird with a strip of bacon and secure with toothpick. Wrap each bird in aluminum foil. Place in shallow baking dish and bake at 300° F. for 2 hours. Remove doves from foil. Return to baking dish. Pour small amount of red wine over each bird and run under broiler until bacon is crisp and brown. Serves 6.

Braised Quail

6 *quail*	1 *bay leaf*
2 *quarts water*	*dash of pepper*
½ *cup salt*	1 *cup halved white grapes*
flour, salt, pepper	1 *teaspoon slivered orange rind*
¼ *cup butter*	6 *slices buttered toast*
1¼ *cups chicken broth*	*grapes and orange slices for*
⅛ *teaspoon thyme*	*garnish*
1 *teaspoon chopped parsley*	

Soak quail in a solution of 2 quarts water and ½ cup salt overnight, or at least 2 to 3 hours. Drain and pat dry. Dredge quail in flour to which salt and pepper have been added; brown in butter in large skillet; remove. Combine chicken broth, thyme, parsley, bay leaf and pepper; pour into skillet. Cover. Simmer 10 minutes; remove bay leaf. Add browned quail, cover and simmer 15 minutes. Add halved grapes and orange rind to skillet. Simmer 5 minutes longer. Place each quail on a toast slice. Garnish with grapes and orange slices and serve with sauce. Serves 6.

Creamed Ham and Chicken

1 *cup chopped fresh mushrooms*	4 *cups diced cooked ham*
2 *green peppers cut into 1-inch*	2 *cups medium-thick cream*
pieces, then blanched	*sauce*
1 *tablespoon melted butter or*	½ *cup sweet cream*
chicken fat	2 *egg yolks, beaten*
1 *boiled fowl, skinned, boned*	1 *can pimientos, drained, cut*
and diced	*into 1-inch slices*

Sauté mushrooms and green peppers in the butter or fat for 5 minutes. Add chicken and ham, then the cream sauce and let simmer until well heated. Season with salt. Combine cream with beaten eggs and add to chicken mixture. Add the pimientos last. Stir well until properly mixed and bring to boiling point only—sauce will curdle if allowed to boil. Serve on toast. Garnish with parsley. Serves 6.

Cornbread Stuffing for Turkey or Chicken

*3 cups corn bread broken into
    small pieces*
*2 cups plain bread crumbs or
    biscuit crumbs*
*1 teaspoon salt
    freshly ground pepper*
1 teaspoon poultry seasoning

1 cup chopped onion
¾ cup chopped celery
½ stick butter
2 eggs
*1 cup chicken broth
    dash of Worcestershire*

Add salt, pepper and poultry seasoning to combined corn bread pieces and crumbs. Lightly brown onion and celery in butter. Add to crumb mixture. Slowly add beaten eggs, then chicken broth and Worcestershire sauce. Mix well. Stuff turkey with dressing. This is ample for a 14- to 16-pound turkey or 2 large hens. Roast fowl as desired.

PART IV

Country Cooking—
Favorite
Family Recipes

Mother Talmadge—a remarkable woman.

1

Mother Talmadge at "Sugar Creek"

MOTHER TALMADGE wouldn't think of buying a frozen vegetable. She depends on her garden-grown varieties and cooks them always with a ham hock or "streak o' lean" bacon.

What she grows, she cooks. Mrs. Eugene Talmadge—I call her Mother Talmadge but almost everyone else calls her "Miss Mitt" —does not believe in spending hours in the kitchen. The garden vegetables boil fine in a large pot. Meat roasts until it is done. Very few recipes are used for the kind of cookin' she does.

She's been in the public limelight ever since she married Eugene Talmadge in 1909. She was the former Mattie Thurmond of Edgefield, South Carolina, cousin of U.S. Senator Strom Thurmond, and came to Georgia as a railroad telegraph operator at Ailey, Georgia, when she was only sixteen. She and Father Talmadge moved to McRae soon after they were married and named their farm "Sugar Creek." She's lived there ever since, managing the farm, and until recent years riding her horse over the 1,400 acres almost daily.

Certainly, Mother Talmadge preferred the farm to the Governor's Mansion where she was transplanted in 1932. The big mansion made of Stone Mountain granite had thirteen rooms and five baths. Determined to bring some of the country to the city, Mother Talmadge brought a cow and kept her in a barn behind the mansion and let her graze on the front lawn. "It was full of onion grass anyway," Mother Talmadge recalls. "We had some nice next-door neighbors who loved buttermilk so I'd take them a gallon or so each week."

They kept three saddle horses there, too. They would ride early in the morning through the wooded area in Ansley Park.

Both Mother Talmadge and I set some sort of records for Georgia First Ladies. I was the youngest and she served the greatest number of terms.

Mother Talmadge was Georgia's First Lady from 1932 until 1936, again returning when her husband was elected a third time in 1940. In 1946, when he was elected Governor for the fourth time, Father Talmadge became ill and died. For thirty years now, Mother Talmadge has remained on the farm, still supervising the kitchen and watching over "Sugar Creek." She is approaching her ninety-seventh birthday.

Mother Talmadge is the real farmer in the Talmadge clan. I believe she has 99 cents out of every dollar she made—or she would have if the Internal Revenue Service hadn't caught up with her. One year when the tax men came around, Herman and I thought our accountant had better go over and help her get her books in order.

The agents finally agreed on the amount of the tax she should pay, and when it was all over, Mother Talmadge fired the accountant.

We asked her why she fired him and she replied, "He didn't know nothing about how to keep me from having to pay taxes."

Three years ago, columnist Celestine Sibley telephoned Mother Talmadge for a story in *The Atlanta Constitution*.

Celestine reported:

It did my heart good to talk to her—a plain, sensible no-nonsense woman now 94 years old. "We're sitting here waiting for rain so we can get our grain planted," she said. "It's time to get rye and oats in the ground." A moment later she mentioned that the kitchen garden had been rewarding this year but it, of course, is on its last legs now. "We did have some collards for dinner today," she mentioned, "and they were mighty good."

To my mind there is nothing so important as freshness when you are cooking, canning and serving vegetables. I like to boil most of the common vegetables we prefer with a ham slice, a streak o' lean or a piece of ham hock. I place the meat in the pan and boil it briskly for a few minutes before adding the vegetables. This is an excellent way to cook turnips, collards, English peas, field peas, lady peas, string beans, pole beans, butter beans, dried butter beans, dried black-eyed peas and so on.

VEGETABLE RECIPES

Collards
Stewed Corn
Spinach Soufflé
Scalloped Squash
Mama's Turnip Greens and
    "Pot Likker"
Beets
Homemade Potato Chips
Black-eyed Peas and Ham Hocks
Hoppin' John
Cabbage
Baked Corn and Tomatoes
Corn Fritters
Scalloped Corn
Stewed Corn
Corn Pudding
Grits #1
Grits #2
Hot Pepper Grits
Baked Eggplant

Fried Eggplant
Fried Okra
Onion Shortcake
Onion-Carrot-Apple Scallop
Onion Surprise
Cottage Potatoes
Stuffed Potatoes
Apple-Squash Dandy
Squash Soufflé
Succotash with Sausage
Sweet Potato Balls
Sweet Potato Pudding
Stewed Tomatoes and Okra
Baked Tomatoes Stuffed with
    Corn
Broiled Tomatoes
'Cile's Fried Tomatoes
Fire-and-Ice Tomatoes
Turnip Greens with Corn Pones
Turnips and Dumplings

Collards (Boiled Greens)

Collards are considered a fall vegetable. Don't pick them until the first frost, we were told. Nowadays, because of cold storage, collards are almost a year-around vegetable. Like turnips, collards should be boiled in water with a piece of ham or bacon for about 1 hour.

1½ pounds collard leaves (stalks removed)	*½ teaspoon salt*
	1 teaspoon sugar
¾ pound of ham skin and trimmings (or a ham hock)	*¼ teaspoon cayenne pepper*
	2 quarts water

Wash leaves in several waters until thoroughly clean. Break into smaller pieces and add ham and seasonings. Cover with about 2 quarts of water and boil until tender. Cook over medium heat for about 1 hour. May be served with sliced beets, chopped onion and vinegar. Serves 6.

Stewed Corn

For 15 or 50 guests use at least 1½ to 2 ears of corn per person, depending on the size of the ears. Using a sharp knife, split each row of kernels and then cut the corn from the cob and scrape the cob for juices. Put kernels and juice in a heavy skillet with a little water, salt and 1 tablespoon sugar. Cook until tender and thickened. Add ½ stick butter and let simmer until butter is melted. Just before serving add ½ cup sweet milk. Serve at once, or reheat if necessary just before bringing to the table.

Spinach Soufflé

3 eggs	*2 pounds fresh spinach, mashed and chopped (or 2 packages frozen spinach, thawed and chopped)*
1 1-pound carton cottage cheese	
⅓ pound Cheddar cheese, grated	

3 tablespoons flour   *salt and pepper*

Beat eggs, add other ingredients and mix well with fork. Pour into greased casserole. Bake for 1 hour at 350° F. Unlike most soufflés, this can be held for a reasonable amount of time without falling. Serves 6 to 8.

Scalloped Squash

6 zucchini or other small squash, sliced in rounds
2 cups diced onion
3 eggs
½ cup evaporated milk
½ stick butter or margarine
¼ cup sugar

½ cup bread crumbs
Worcestershire sauce (dash)
1 teaspoon salt
dash black pepper
grated Parmesan cheese
paprika (dash)

Cover squash and onion with water and simmer over medium heat until tender. Drain in colander. Mash thoroughly and add eggs, milk, melted butter, sugar, bread crumbs, Worcestershire sauce, salt and pepper. Pour into buttered baking dish. Top with enough grated cheese to cover. Sprinkle paprika lightly over top and bake in 350° F. oven until mixture is firm and cheese is thoroughly melted. Serves 6 to 8.

Mama's Turnip Greens and "Pot Likker"

3 cups water
2 pounds turnip greens

1 small ham hock
6 small turnips, diced

Simmer together for 30 minutes the water, greens and ham hock. Add diced turnips to simmer with leaves and ham hock for about 30 minutes more. Serve greens and turnips in liquor. Or serve liquor separately in small cups. Corn bread may be used for dipping in liquor if desired. Besides tasting good, the liquor is full of vitamins. Serves 6.

Beets

¼ *cup sugar*
1 *tablespoon flour*
cold water
1 *cup hot water*

¼ *cup vinegar*
½ *teaspoon salt*
1 *tablespoon butter*
3 *cups cooked sliced beets*

Mix sugar and flour and add a little cold water to make a paste. Add hot water slowly. Stir and cook until thickened. Add vinegar, salt and butter. Add beets and allow to stand over low heat to develop flavor and to color sauce. Serves 6.

Homemade Potato Chips

With no preservatives and as salt-free as you wish, homemade potato chips are fun to make and good to eat. Use new potatoes and peel with a potato peeler. Cut paper thin with your sharpest knife. Set a heavy skillet over medium heat. Add mild vegetable oil to a depth of 1½ inches. Heat oil until hot but not smoking. Drop potato slices into hot oil one at a time. Do not overlap. Cover bottom of skillet with potato slices. When they are light brown, turn over. When brown on both sides, remove and drain on paper towels. Salt to taste and serve hot or cold.

Black-eyed Peas and Ham Hocks

1 *smoked ham hock, about 1
pound*
1 *cup dried black-eyed peas*
½ *cup coarsely chopped onions*

1 *medium-size celery stalk,
coarsely chopped*
freshly ground black pepper

Place the ham hock in a heavy pot. Add enough water to cover. Bring to a boil over high heat, reduce to low and simmer, partially covered, for 2 hours. Wash the peas in a colander under cold running water.

Add peas, onions, celery, and black pepper to the pot, mix well, and bring to a boil again. Reduce to low and simmer, partially covered, for 1½ hours. Serves 4.

Hoppin' John

2 *cups dried black-eyed peas*
1 *cup raw rice*
1 *ham hock or 3 tablespoons*
   bacon drippings

3 *cups water*
  salt to taste

Boil black-eyed peas until tender. Add rice, ham hock or bacon drippings, salt and enough water to steam rice. Cook over low burner for 1 hour.

Cabbage

1 *medium head cabbage*
  milk
2 *tablespoons butter*

1 *teaspoon sugar*
  salt
  freshly ground pepper

Cut cabbage fine and wash in cold water. Soak for ½ hour. Place in saucepan with water to cover and cook until barely tender. This will take only a few minutes. Drain and place in baking dish with enough milk to cover it. Add butter, sugar, salt and pepper. Mix. Bake at 300° F. until top is light brown. Serves 4 to 6.

Baked Corn and Tomatoes

2 *cups cooked corn*
2 *cups tomatoes*
1 *teaspoon sugar*

1 *teaspoon salt*
1 *cup bread crumbs*
1 *tablespoon butter*

Mix first 4 ingredients and place in buttered baking dish. Cover with crumbs. Dot with butter and bake at 350° F. for 30 minutes. Serves 4 to 5.

Corn Fritters

1 cup sifted flour	*5 tablespoons milk*
1 teaspoon baking power	*1 tablespoon melted fat*
½ teaspoon salt	*1⅔ cups fresh-cut corn*
4 tablespoons sugar	*fat for frying*
1 egg	

Sift dry ingredients together. Beat eggs. Add milk and melted fat. Add to dry ingredients. Beat until smooth. Stir in corn. Let stand 5 to 10 minutes. Heat fat for frying. Drop by tablespoons into hot fat. Fry until brown. Drain on absorbent paper. Serve hot. Makes 24 fritters.

Scalloped Corn

8 ears fresh corn	*salt*
bread crumbs	*freshly ground pepper*
butter	*milk*

Cut corn from cob. Put a layer of corn in a baking dish, cover with bread crumbs and dot with butter, salt and pepper. Alternate these layers until dish is full. Add milk to moisten. Sprinkle crumbs on top. Bake at 300° F. for 30 minutes. Serves 6.

Stewed Corn

8 ears corn	*1 tablespoon butter*
water	*salt*
1 cup milk	*freshly ground pepper*

Cut corn from cob with sharp knife; scrape cob to extract juice and remaining pulp. Put corn and any pulp and juices in a saucepan with water barely to cover and cook gently for 20 minutes. Add milk, butter, salt and pepper. Cook until it thickens. Serves 6.

Corn Pudding

4 or 5 ears of corn (white corn is good; young field corn even better)
2 eggs
1 cup milk

2 tablespoons sugar
3 tablespoons melted butter
½ teaspoon salt
⅛ teaspoon pepper

Cut corn off cob with a sharp knife, then scrape out the tender inside kernels with back edge of a dull knife. Add eggs, which have been beaten with the milk. Add rest of ingredients. Pour into a greased baking dish and bake in a 375° F. oven until pudding is just set—if it does not shake when moved, it is ready. This takes 35 to 45 minutes. Serves 4 to 5.

The slaves did not prepare their vegetables haphazardly. As reported by Lizzie Farmer, an ex-slave of Texas, their method required care and patience. They began by putting a piece of hog jowl in a pot and then added beans. When the beans were half done, they added "a mess of cabbage," and when the cabbage was half done, put in squash. When the squash was half done, they added okra. The vegetables, when cooked through, would be removed a layer at a time. With less time to fuss, they would cook field peas, for which they had considerable enthusiasm, heavily seasoned with red pepper.

—from Roll, Jordan, Roll, *Eugene D. Genovese, Vintage Books, Random House, New York, 1972, p. 548.*

The new popularity of grits has certainly brought the country to the city. I could hardly believe it when **The New York Times** *devoted half a page to grits. Craig Claiborne had even researched the origin of the word, telling us it stems from "a Middle English word* gryt *meaning bran and from the Old English* grytt."

My own Baked Cheese Grits recipe (p. 27) is a favorite among my family and friends. I claim to have converted many a Yankee to liking grits because of that recipe. Served plain or with cheese, grits are best enjoyed on a plate with country ham, scrambled eggs and red-eye gravy.

There are still a few places you can buy home-ground speckled heart grits (Callaway Gardens in Georgia always has them). The speckled appearance of these grits comes from grinding the whole-grain product, including the heart of the corn, which is the most vitamin-rich part of the entire kernel.

Grits #1 (Plain or Speckled)

1 cup grits
4 cups boiling water

1 teaspoon salt
4 tablespoons butter

Add grits gradually to boiling salted water and bring again to a boil, stirring. Reduce heat to medium, cover and cook for 20 to 30 minutes, stirring often to prevent sticking. Additional water (or a little milk) may be added to reach the desired consistency. Before serving, stir in butter. Serves 4.

Grits #2 (Fried)

2 cups cooked grits (leftover)
2 eggs

bacon drippings

Place leftover grits in tall tumbler. They will "congeal" overnight. Remove from glass. They will be molded into a firmly set cylinder.

Slice into 1/4-inch rounds. Beat eggs well. Dip slices in beaten eggs. Fry in bacon drippings, turning once. Serves 4.

Hot Pepper Grits

1½ cups grits
5 cups water
1½ teaspoons salt
1 pound grated sharp cheese
1 stick margarine or butter

3 eggs, well beaten
1 small can pimiento, chopped
2 tablespoons chopped green
  chili peppers

Cook grits in salted water until done, following directions for Grits #1 (p. 166). Add rest of ingredients and mix well. Put into greased baking dish or casserole and bake for 1 hour at 300° F. Serves 10.

Baked Eggplant

3 medium-size eggplants
3 slices bread
3 eggs
3 tablespoons butter

salt
freshly ground pepper
bread crumbs

Boil eggplants, peeled and cut up, until tender. Drain, reserving enough liquid to soak about 3 slices of bread. Mash eggplant into a pulp. Beat eggs, mix with the mashed eggplant and bread. Add butter, salt and pepper to taste. Put in buttered baking dish and bake at 300° F. for 1 hour. Before serving, sprinkle toasted bread crumbs over top, dot with butter and put back in oven for a few minutes. Serves 8.

Fried Eggplant

2 medium-size eggplants
salt and pepper to taste
2 eggs, beaten

1/4 cup milk
1/2 cup cracker crumbs
1/2 cup shortening

Peel and slice eggplant in ½-inch slices. Season. Dip each slice in mixture of egg and milk and then into cracker crumbs. Heat fat in skillet until very hot. Fry eggplant slices until brown and crisp, approximately 10 minutes for both sides. You may have to add fat. Drain and serve hot. Serves 6.

Fried Okra

2 *pounds small okra*　　　　½ *cup cornmeal*
½ *teaspoon salt*　　　　　　*4 tablespoons bacon drippings*
⅛ *teaspoon pepper*　　　　　　*or mild vegetable oil*

Wash okra well, drain, and cut off tip and stem ends. Cut okra crosswise into pieces ½ inch thick. Season slices with salt and pepper; **roll** in cornmeal. Sauté well in hot bacon drippings or oil until tender and golden brown on both sides. Serves 8.

Onion Shortcake

6 *medium-size onions*　　　　*3 cups self-rising cornmeal*
4 *tablespoons butter or*　　　　*4 tablespoons shortening*
　　margarine　　　　　　　*1 cup milk*
½ *teaspoon salt*　　　　　　　*2 eggs*
½ *teaspoon pepper*　　　　　　*paprika*

Sauté onions in butter until they begin to turn yellow and are somewhat translucent. Sprinkle with salt and pepper. Mix cornmeal with shortening, add milk, and stir. Pour this batter into greased deep pie dish to a thickness of about ½ inch. Spoon the cooked onions evenly over the top. Beat eggs until frothy and pour over the onions. Sprinkle with paprika. Bake for 30 minutes at 400° F. or until golden brown. Serve warm, cut into wedges. Serves 8.

Onion-Carrot-Apple Scallop

2 *cups sliced onions*
1 *cup diced carrots*
1 *cup diced apples*
¼ *cup water*

4 *tablespoons butter*
salt
freshly ground black pepper

Place all ingredients in baking dish in layers, cover and bake at 350° **F.** for 1 hour. Excellent with roast pork. Serves 4.

Onion Surprise

½ *cup beef bouillon*
6 *large onions*
salt

freshly ground pepper
½ *cup chopped, toasted pecans*
½ *cup grated sharp cheese*

Bring bouillon to a boil. Slice onions into ½-inch-thick rounds and add to bouillon. Cover. Simmer for 10 to 12 minutes. Salt and pepper to taste. Mix pecans with cheese. Add to the onions. Shake the pan well for a minute or two in order to mix cheese and pecans with onions. Transfer to a heated serving dish. Serves 6.

Cottage Potatoes

10 *large potatoes*
½ *pound American cheese, diced*
1 *pound onions, diced*
1 *green pepper, diced*
2 *slices bread, diced*

1 *small can pimientos, diced*
salt and pepper to taste
corn flakes, crushed
½ *cup melted butter*
milk to moisten

Cook potatoes in jackets until tender. Set aside to cool. Remove jackets and dice. Combine all diced ingredients and mix well in large bowl. Season to taste. Pour mixture into a shallow 8 × 12-inch baking dish and cover with crushed corn flakes. Pour melted butter over all and add enough milk to moisten. Bake in 350° F. oven for 1 hour or until golden brown. Serves 8 to 10.

Stuffed Potatoes

baking potatoes (allow 1 medium
   per person)
milk
butter

salt
freshly ground pepper
sharp cheese, grated

Wash potatoes. Bake until soft. Cover with damp cloth for a few minutes. Cut about 2 inches off tops. Scoop out interior and reserve skins. Add scalded milk, butter, salt and pepper to potatoes. Beat well until smooth. Fill each skin with potato mixture. Sprinkle with grated cheese. Return to oven for 10 minutes to heat through.

Apple-Squash Dandy

3 pounds yellow squash, peeled
   and cubed
1 large onion, chopped
   butter
3 cooking apples

1 teaspoon salt
3 tablespoons brown sugar
1 teaspoon cinnamon
½ cup chopped and toasted
   pecans

Sauté squash and onions briefly in butter. Cover pan and cook, stirring occasionally, until squash is almost tender. Add sliced, *unpeeled* cooking apples, salt, brown sugar and cinnamon. Cook until squash and apples are tender. Stir in pecans just before serving. Serves 8 to 10.

Squash Soufflé

4 tablespoons butter
2 tablespoons flour
1 cup milk
2 cups cooked squash
2 teaspoons finely cut onion

1½ teaspoons salt
⅛ teaspoon black pepper
2 eggs, separated
¾ cup cracker crumbs

Melt the butter; add flour and blend. Gradually add milk, stirring constantly. Cook over low heat until sauce is thick. Remove from heat. Drain squash thoroughly and mash. Add onion, salt, pepper, egg yolk and cracker crumbs. Add sauce and mix together lightly. Fold in stiffly beaten egg whites. Pour into buttered baking dish and bake in 350° F. oven until firm. Serves 6.

Succotash with Sausage

1 pound country sausage links
2 large tomatoes
1½ cups whole okra
1½ cups butter beans
1½ cups corn kernels

1 cup tomato juice
1½ teaspoons salt
freshly ground pepper
1½ cups rice

Brown sausage on all sides in a large skillet (prick skins before cooking to prevent bursting). Pour off excess fat. Peel tomatoes and chop coarsely. Add to skillet, including any juice. Add okra, beans and corn. Mix well. Add tomato juice. Sprinkle with salt and pepper. Cover skillet, reduce heat and simmer 25 minutes. Cook rice separately. Serve succotash over rice. Serves 6.

Sweet Potato Balls

2 cups sweet potatoes
3 tablespoons butter or margarine

salt and pepper to taste
1 cup peanuts or pecans, crushed fine

Mash hot potatoes with melted butter, adding salt and pepper. Shape into small balls and roll in crushed peanuts or pecans. Place on a buttered cookie sheet in a 300° F. oven to heat through. Serves 8 to 10.

Sweet Potato Pudding

1½ *cups milk*
  2 *cups grated raw sweet*
    potatoes
  2 *eggs*

1 *cup sugar*
2 *teaspoons vanilla*
  dash of salt
½ *stick butter, melted*

Pour milk over potatoes immediately after grating to hold golden color of potatoes. Mix together eggs, sugar, vanilla and salt. Add potatoes, milk and butter. Beat together thoroughly. Pour mixture into baking dish and bake uncovered at 350° F. for 90 minutes. Serves 6.

Stewed Tomatoes and Okra

1 *tablespoon bacon drippings*
1 *pound okra, cut in pieces (or*
  1 *10-ounce package frozen*
  okra)
4 *fresh tomatoes, cut in pieces (or*
  1 *16-ounce can tomatoes)*

1 *onion, chopped*
1 *teaspoon Worcestershire sauce*
  salt and pepper to taste
½ *teaspoon sugar*

Heat bacon drippings in frying pan and add okra, stirring over medium heat until, as 'Cile says, "the slime goes away." Add tomatoes, onion, Worcestershire, salt, pepper and sugar. Continue to cook until tomatoes and onion are tender. Cover and keep warm until ready to serve. *Do not add water to this dish.* Serves 4 to 5.

Baked Tomatoes Stuffed with Corn

6 *large ripe red tomatoes*
½ *cup stewed corn*
½ *onion, diced*

½ *cup chopped sweet pepper*
  (optional)
  salt and pepper to taste

Cut slice from top of tomatoes and scoop pulp out with a spoon. Mix pulp with corn, onion and peppers (if used). Add salt and pepper.

Carefully place tomatoes in greased baking dish. Fill with mixture. Bake in 375° F. oven for approximately 30 minutes. Serves 6.

Broiled Tomatoes

3 large ripe tomatoes　　　　*2 teaspoons butter*
　salt to taste　　　　　　　*2 tablespoons fine dry bread*
　freshly ground pepper　　　　*crumbs*

Wash tomatoes; cut off stem ends. Cut into 1-inch slices. Place slices on broiler rack. Sprinkle with salt and pepper. Dot each slice with butter and sprinkle with bread crumbs. Broil until tomatoes are soft and crumbs lightly browned, about 7 minutes. Serves 6.

'Cile's Fried Tomatoes

When 'Cile prepares tomatoes for frying, she cuts them so thin that Herman says, "'Cile should have been a surgeon." She places them in ice water to keep them crisp until all are cut and ready to fry.

6 to 8 very firm tomatoes, thinly　　*1 teaspoon sugar*
　sliced　　　　　　　　　　*salt and pepper to taste*
　flour (or cornmeal)　　　　　*fat for frying*

Drain tomatoes in colander and dip one by one in flour or cornmeal mixed with sugar, salt and pepper. Gently put them in deep hot fat for about 1 minute to brown. Take out and lay them on paper towels to drain. Serve immediately or, for serving later, reheat on an ovenproof platter. Serves 6 to 8.

Variation: Slice partly ripe tomatoes thick. Salt, pepper and sprinkle with flour. Place them in a skillet with hot butter or margarine and fry lightly on both sides. Remove. Make a gravy of 1 cup milk, a teaspoon butter or margarine and 1 tablespoon flour. Heat through and pour over tomatoes.

Fire-and-Ice Tomatoes

6 large ripe, firm tomatoes,
   peeled and quartered

1 green pepper, cut in strips
1 red onion, sliced into rings

Arrange vegetables attractively in a serving dish.

SAUCE

⅔ cup vinegar
1½ teaspoons celery salt
1½ teaspoons mustard seed
½ teaspoon salt

4½ teaspoons sugar
⅛ teaspoon red pepper
⅓ cup water
⅛ teaspoon black pepper

Combine all ingredients. Bring to boil and boil furiously for 1 minute. While still hot, pour over the vegetables. Cool. Just before serving, add 1 peeled sliced cucumber.

   This keeps, refrigerated (without the cucumber), for several days. Serves 6.

Turnip Greens with Corn Pones

1 ham hock
1 bunch turnip greens
1 cup cornmeal

½ teaspoon baking powder
1 teaspoon salt
2 tablespoons bacon drippings

Boil ham hock in water for 15 minutes. Add well-washed turnip greens and cook until tender.

   To make the pones, combine cornmeal, baking powder, salt and bacon drippings. Add enough warm water to hold batter together when rolled into pones.

   Drain greens of excess water. Place pones on top of greens, cover and steam until done, turning pones once. Serves 6.

Turnips and Dumplings

2 *quarts turnip greens*	½ *cup flour*
1 *pound turnips*	1 *teaspoon baking powder*
2 *quarts boiling water*	1 *teaspoon sugar*
1 *ham hock or a piece of salt*	½ *teaspoon salt*
pork with rind	3 *tablespoons butter or*
1 *teaspoon salt*	*margarine, melted*
1½ *cups white cornmeal*	1 *egg, beaten*

Wash greens thoroughly. Pare and dice turnips. Bring 2 quarts water to boil in large kettle. Add ham hock or salt pork, greens, turnips and 1 teaspoon salt. Cover, simmer for 2 hours. Remove 1 cup "pot likker" for use in dumpling.

For the dumplings, stir together cornmeal, flour, baking powder, sugar and ½ teaspoon salt; stir in butter or margarine and the 1 cup "pot likker." Stir in egg. With a spoon, drop 1 tablespoon at a time onto simmering greens. Cover and simmer for 30 minutes. Serves 6 to 8.

White Southerners dreadfully overcooked their vegetables and threw away the liquid, which contained most of the nutritional value. They thought that vegetables had to be cooked "thoroughly," and thus made a great contribution to one of the worst features of our national cuisine. The slaves followed suit but with a difference: they highly valued the liquid and drank it. As a result of their penchant for this "pot-likker" (or pot-liquor or pot-licker), they probably gained much more value from their method of preparation than did the whites, except for those poorer whites who copied them.

—*from* Roll, Jordan, Roll, *Eugene D. Genovese, Vintage Books, Random House, New York, 1972, p. 547.*

2

Aunt Lillie's "House by the Road"

If there is such a thing as a "country gourmet" cook, I can claim kin on my side of the family. My Aunt Lillie Shingler captivated Duncan Hines with her cooking down in Ashburn, Georgia. Aunt Lillie was born in Charleston, South Carolina. Even though she has lived in Ashburn for over sixty-five years, if you ask her where she's from, she will say "Charleston."

The depression put Aunt Lillie and Uncle Bob Shingler *into* business. They turned their family home into a tourist lodge on old U.S. 41. That was the main highway through southern Georgia. Her "guests," as she called the tourists who stopped overnight, were given delicious home-cooked meals in the dining room. As her culinary reputation grew, so did the number of "guests." She and Uncle Bob would keep adding rooms to the house. It was before the days of the term "motel." They called it simply "The House by the Road."

"WIREGRASS FARMER"

One time Duncan Hines heard about the fine food served there and stopped in. After sampling her famous waffles, apple casseroles, sweet potato soufflé and Guinea Squash Pie (which is really eggplant with a Charleston title), he put his stamp of approval on "The House by the Road." He would stop whenever he came south, and, when he published his famous book of recipes, four of Aunt Lillie's were included.

Here are the recipes from Aunt Lillie's kitchen that Duncan Hines included in his *Adventures in Good Cooking*.

DUNCAN HINES BORROWS AUNT LILLIE'S RECIPES

Waffles

INGREDIENTS
- 2 *egg yolks*
- 1 *cup milk*
- 1½ *cups cake flour—sifted*
- 2 *teaspoons sugar*
- 1 *teaspoon salt*
- ¼ *cup butter—melted*

DIRECTIONS
Stir to a smooth batter.

- 2 *egg whites—beaten stiff*
- 2 *teaspoons baking powder*

Fold in eggs and baking powder.

Sweet Potato Soufflé

Serves 8

INGREDIENTS
- 6 *sweet potatoes, medium size*

DIRECTIONS
Peel and boil in salted water until tender. Put through a potato ricer and mash thoroughly.

- 2 *egg yolks—beaten*
- ½ *cup milk*

Mix together.

177

INGREDIENTS (*cont.*)

½ *cup sugar*
½ *cup raisins*
  1 teaspoon nutmeg
  3 tablespoons melted butter

  2 egg whites—beaten
  1 tablespoon sugar
  *1 teaspoon lemon juice or
     orange juice*

DIRECTIONS (*cont.*)

Add to egg mixture and stir in mashed potatoes.

Put in buttered casserole and bake in 350° F. oven for about 30 minutes, or until light brown on top and bottom.

Make a meringue and place on top and put under broiler a few minutes to brown.

Apple Sauce

Serves 8

INGREDIENTS

  8 medium apples—tart
¼ *cup water*

½ *cup sugar*
  1 teaspoon butter
  1 teaspoon nutmeg

  1 dozen marshmallows

DIRECTIONS

Peel and cut in large pieces. Cook and drain and put in bowl.

Add sugar, butter and nutmeg to apples.

Put apples in baking dish and cover with marshmallows, stick in oven until brown.

Guinea Squash Pie

Serves 6

INGREDIENTS

  1 eggplant—medium size

  *3 slices toasted bread
     little milk*

DIRECTIONS

Peel and boil eggplant in salted water. When done drain and mash.

Soak bread until soft. Mix with mashed eggplant.

INGREDIENTS *(cont.)*

2 *eggs—beaten slightly*

1 *onion—chopped*
3 *tablespoons of melted butter*
1 *teaspoon salt*
  pepper to taste

2 *tablespoons cream*

DIRECTIONS *(cont.)*

Add to above mixture.

Blend in with mixture and put in buttered casserole.

Put over top and bake in 350° F. oven for 25 minutes until a golden brown.

CASSEROLES AND COVERED DISHES

Asparagus Casserole
Carter Family Eggplant Casserole
Cheese Soufflé
Chicken and Rice Casserole
Fresh Corn Casserole
Pork and Black-eyed Peas
  Casserole

Leftover Ham and Chicken
  Casserole
Ham and Vegetable Casserole
Mushroom and Rice Casserole
Red Beans and Rice
Squash and Canadian Bacon
Three-P's "Covered" Dish

Asparagus Casserole

1 *pound fresh asparagus or 1*
  #2 can asparagus spears
1¼ *cup rolled cracker crumbs*
1 *pimiento, chopped*
3 *eggs, beaten*
1 *cup grated sharp cheese*

1 *cup milk*
1 *teaspoon salt*
⅛ *teaspoon Tabasco sauce*
¼ *cup butter or margarine,*
  melted

Break tough ends off fresh asparagus. Wash asparagus and cook until tender (or drain canned asparagus spears). Sprinkle half the cracker crumbs on the bottom of an oiled casserole. Add asparagus. Mix the rest of the ingredients except butter or margarine and pour over cracker crumbs and asparagus. Pour butter over all, and sprinkle remainder of cracker crumbs on top. Bake at 350° F. for 30 minutes. Serves 4.

Carter Family
Eggplant Casserole

Rosalynn Carter has given us the best definition of Southern hospitality:* "I don't think that lavish entertaining is what Southern hospitality is all about. To me, what it is, and always has been, is simply a genuinely warm welcome to anyone who drops in. People in the South really enjoy having company, even when it is unexpected. And, because we truly enjoy it, people always feel welcome." Here's a vegetable dish she loves to serve.

1 large peeled eggplant, cut into 8 circles	*2 cups chopped, peeled fresh tomatoes*
1 teaspoon salt	*pinch of thyme*
½ teaspoon pepper	*salt and pepper*
3 tablespoons butter or margarine	*¼ cup chopped parsley*
1 cup chopped onion	*½ cup white bread crumbs*
2 cloves minced garlic	*1 cup grated Swiss, Gruyère or mozzarella cheese*

Slice eggplant about 1 inch thick, trimming slices so they are all approximately same size. Place in oiled shallow ovenproof dish. Sprinkle with salt and pepper. Broil 5 minutes or until fork tender. Heat the butter; add onion and garlic. Cook until yellow. Add tomatoes and trimmings of eggplant; cook until thick. Stir in seasonings, parsley and bread crumbs. Correct seasoning. Pile on the broiled eggplant. Cover with cheese. Bake at 350° F. until cheese is melted.

Cheese Soufflé

4 slices of bread, cubed, crusts removed	*2 cups milk*
¾ pound sharp Cheddar cheese, grated	*½ teaspoon salt*
	¼ teaspoon dry mustard
4 eggs, beaten	*2 tablespoons sherry*

* *McCalls,* February 1977.

Butter a straight-sided baking dish. Alternate layers of bread cubes with cheese. Mix eggs, milk, salt, mustard and wine together. Pour over bread and cheese layers. If serving for lunch, prepare the night before. If serving for dinner, prepare early in the morning. An hour before serving, set dish in pan of water and bake in 350° F. oven for 50 to 60 minutes. Remove from water and leave dish in oven a few minutes more to be sure bottom is done. Serves 5.

Chicken and Rice Casserole

½ stick butter
 1 young chicken, cut in pieces
   salt and pepper to taste
 4 large onions, sliced
½ cup fresh mushrooms, sautéed,
   or 1 4-ounce can mushrooms,
   drained (save liquid)

2 chicken bouillon cubes
 1 cup raw rice

Melt butter in casserole. Place chicken, seasoned with salt and pepper, in casserole in layers with onions and mushrooms. Bake, covered, for 1½ hours at 350° F. Remove chicken, add enough boiling water to mushroom liquid (if you have any—otherwise plain water will do) to make 4½ cups of broth in casserole. Dissolve bouillon cubes in broth. Add rice. Replace chicken and bake, covered, for 1 hour more. Serves 4.

Fresh Corn Casserole

6 slices bacon
 8 ears fresh corn, cut from cob
   and cob scraped for juices
¾ cup chopped green pepper

½ cup chopped onion
 1 teaspoon salt
½ teaspoon pepper
 2 tomatoes, peeled and sliced

In a large skillet, cook bacon until browned. Remove from skillet, drain on paper towels and crumble. Remove all but 2 tablespoons bacon fat from skillet. Add corn, green pepper and onion to skillet. Cook over high heat for 5 minutes. Add crumbled bacon, salt and pepper. In a 2-quart casserole, alternate layers of the corn mixture and tomato slices. Bake uncovered in 350° F. oven 30 to 40 minutes. Serves 6.

Pork and Black-eyed Peas Casserole

1 boneless smoked pork butt, about 2 pounds	*2 cups water*
1 tablespoon mixed pickling spices	*1 cup chicken stock*
	1 garlic clove, chopped
¼ cup brown sugar	*1 cup coarsely chopped onion*
1½ pounds frozen black-eyed peas	*1 bay leaf*
1 cup tomato juice	*freshly ground pepper*
	1 teaspoon salt

Place meat, pickling spices and sugar in a deep kettle; add hot water to cover. Bring to a boil; reduce heat to low and simmer for 1 hour. Let stand in cooking liquid while preparing peas.

Combine peas with rest of ingredients. Bring to a rapid boil. Reduce heat to low, simmer for 30 minutes. Remove peas with liquid in which they cooked to a 2½-quart casserole dish; place drained pork butt in peas. Cover and bake at 350° F. for 30 minutes. Remove pork butt from casserole and slice before serving. Arrange slices in center of casserole. Serves 6.

Leftover Ham and Chicken Casserole

½ pound cooked ham, diced	*1 tablespoon sugar*
1 tablespoon chopped onion	*1 cup diced American cheese*
2 cups Basic Cream Sauce (p. 26) or 1 can (10 ounces) condensed cream of chicken soup and ½ cup milk	*1 cup cooked, diced chicken*
	3 cups bread cubes
	2 tablespoons melted butter

Brown ham in skillet. Brown onion in same skillet. Combine with sauce or soup and milk. Heat until blended. Add sugar, cheese and chicken. Combine with ham and onions in casserole. Scatter bread cubes over. Drizzle with butter. Bake at 350° F. for 30 minutes. Serves 4.

Ham and Vegetable Casserole

2 *cups diced or ground ham*
1 *cup thinly sliced potatoes*
1 *cup thinly sliced carrots*
½ *cup chopped celery*
½ *cup mushrooms*
   salt and pepper to taste

1 *cup Basic Cream Sauce*
   (p. 26)
parsley

Fill a casserole dish with layers of ham, potatoes, carrots, celery, mushrooms. Season with salt and pepper. Cover with cream sauce. Bake uncovered at 350° F. for 1½ hours. Serve bubbly hot, garnished with parsley sprigs. Serves 6.

Mushroom and Rice Casserole

This goes particularly well with both ham and chicken. It can be prepared in advance for large parties, baked for half the time indicated and then placed in freezer, ready when needed.

½ *cup mild vegetable oil*
2 *eggs, beaten*
4 *cups cooked rice*
1 *small can evaporated milk*
1½ *cups grated sharp Cheddar*
   cheese

½ *cup mushrooms*
1 *large onion*
2 *cups Basic Cream Sauce*
   (p. 26)
salt and pepper to taste

Add oil to beaten eggs. Combine with all other ingredients. Place in 3-quart baking dish. Bake for 1 hour in 350° F. oven. Serves 12.

Red Beans and Rice

1 ham bone	*3 tablespoons oil*
1½ cups water	*½ pound ham, cubed*
2 teaspoons garlic salt	*¼ pound hot sausage, sliced*
¼ teaspoon Tabasco sauce	*½ pound smoked sausage, sliced*
1 teaspoon Worcestershire sauce	*2 bay leaves*
	salt to taste
1 pound red beans, washed	*freshly ground pepper*
1 cup chopped celery	*½ cup chopped parsley*
1 cup chopped onions	*2 cups cooked rice*
1½ clove garlic, minced	

In a large pot or Dutch oven, place ham bone, water, garlic salt, Tabasco, Worcestershire and beans. Cook, uncovered, over low flame. Sauté celery, onions and garlic in oil until transparent. Add to beans. In another pan sauté ham and both kinds of sausage. Drain. Add cooked meats, bay leaves, salt and pepper to beans. Continue to cook over low flame until beans are soft and creamy—approximately 2½ hours. Remove bay leaves and add parsley before serving. For additional thickness cook longer. Serve over hot, fluffy rice. Serves 6.

Squash and Canadian Bacon

2 pounds squash, cubed or sliced	*¼ cup brown sugar*
¾ cup fresh cranberries, halved	*½ teaspoon cinnamon*
¼ cup coarsely chopped pecans	*6 slices Canadian-style bacon,*
¼ cup granulated sugar	*½ inch thick*

Cook squash, drain, and combine with cranberries, pecans, sugars and cinnamon. Pour into greased casserole. Top with bacon slices. Bake at 350° F. for 45 minutes. Serves 6.

Three-P's "Covered" Dish

1 cup crushed pineapple
3 eggs, beaten
1 pound mashed sweet potatoes
4 tablespoons brown sugar
5 tablespoons peanut butter
  dash of salt

½ cup miniature marshmallows
¼ cup chopped dry-roasted
  peanuts

Drain pineapple. In blender, mix with eggs, sweet potatoes, brown sugar, peanut butter and salt. Or whip by hand. Pour into 8 × 8-inch buttered pan. Top with marshmallows and peanuts. Bake at 350° F. until heated through and marshmallows are melted and lightly browned. Serves 8.

THE NASHVILLE TRADITION

"In the main, Nashville cookery remains true to its traditions. The baked ham which so charmed LaFayette when he had lunch at the Hermitage in 1825 still charms the discriminating diners among us. The turnip greens which became a favorite in the 1840's have lost none of their desirability in twelve decades. Corn bread had so established itself by 1880 that it was one of the prime exhibits of the Centennial held that year. Corn bread remains one of our staffs of life."

—*from the Junior League of Nashville's Foreword to* Nashville Seasons, *by Dr. Alfred Leland Crabb.*

3

Grandfather Shingler's "Sparrow Nest Farm"

AUNT LILLIE'S "HOUSE BY THE ROAD" was one of a cluster of three houses in Ashburn owned by members of my family. I grew up in the house next door. My grandparents' home—"Sparrow Nest Farm"—is just across U.S. 41.

I've often wondered why Grandfather James Simon Shingler named his Victorian house for the sparrow, of all birds, but I didn't question it when he was still around to tell me.

Some say I inherited my interest in business from Grandpa Shingler. Because of the pine forests around Ashburn, turpentine "stills" were big business, as were the naval stores which sold the products. Grandfather Shingler made a fortune—and lost it—in this business. I remember as a child that people referred to the time when he was listed in Dun and Bradstreet at $1.5 million, which was a vast amount of money then.

His fortune disappeared around the time of the Depression, but it didn't keep him from creating a new "business." He and Grandmother Emma set up a roadside pecan stand. They sold home-cured country hams, too. Grandfather would hang hams and bags of pecans and peanuts from his stand at the side of U.S. 41. You might call his stand an "Early Stuckey's" on the well-traveled roadway through Georgia to Florida.

Long before I had ever heard the Talmadge name, I was exposed to politics. My grandfather served in the State Senate a number of years. And my father, Clinton Shingler, was Mayor of Ashburn until he died of pneumonia at the age of forty-two. I was

"WIREGRASS FARMER"

only nine at the time, and I remember how abruptly my charmed life as the Mayor's only daughter ended. No more exciting public appearances. No more free tickets to county fairs and other such events.

Father had been a successful businessman and a popular mayor. He left Mother with an insurance income of $125 per month, a lovely house with good farm acreage, and four growing children to raise through the Great Depression and after. Fortunately, Mother had graduated from Fairmont College in Washington, D.C., and knew how to manage both money and children.

Mother (Stella) is now eighty-seven. Probably because she is a country doctor's daughter, she has always been interested in matters of health. As we were growing up, she saw to it that we always had a balanced diet. She was a "natural foods" cook long before anyone had ever thought of the term. She would be sure we ate all of our vegetables and drank our turnip "pot likker" served hot in a cup before we would get our favorite boiled-custard ice cream, which we had helped her make by cranking the freezer.

At the time, I wasn't too conscious of the strain the Depression must have put on Mama and the other older folks. My three brothers and I had a good swimming pond, which Grandfather Shingler called "Sparrow Nest Lake," and ponies to ride. "Mr. Tom" McKenzie, who was a sort of father to me after my own father died, planted a cane patch for us near his barn. After school we'd saddle up and ride over to his place, cut a stalk of cane and peel and chew it, sitting on the fence. That is when "Mr. Tom's" daughter, Carolyn (McKenzie) Carter, and I became close friends.

Saturday afternoons we'd get dressed in our best and go to town. Usually this meant sitting in the drugstore and ordering a Coke which could be decorated with an olive or a lime slice or a cherry —or all three, if you wished—for five cents. There was a little hamburger stand run by the only local hairdresser in part of an automobile garage. Older people would come to town on Saturdays, park their cars on one of the two business streets in Ashburn then —the Front and the Back Street—and they'd sit for hours watching people walk by.

The first time I ate any foods other than strictly Georgia cooking was when Tom McKenzie learned to make Italian spaghetti. Carolyn's father got the recipe from a friend in Atlanta who knew a man who owned an Italian restaurant. I doubt anyone in Ashburn had ever had *real* Italian spaghetti sauce until then. "Mr. Tom" would cook the sauce all day. After absorbing those aromas Carolyn and I could hardly wait until supper.

"Mr. Tom" had a fishing camp at Cherry Lake near Valdosta. He would take crowds of us young people there for weekends, filling us up with catfish chowder and delicious hush puppies. "Mr. Tom's" brother Gordon married my Aunt Clyde, so they blended the good recipes from the Shingler family with those of the McKenzies. Aunt Clyde specialized in mustard relish, which she gave away each year at Christmas. She had it on the table at every meal.

The McKenzie men liked to cook. I remember "Mr. Tom's" wife, Hallie, saying she'd really prefer doing it herself to cleaning up after "Mr. Tom" made one of his special dishes.

My Aunt Louise Cannon now lives at "Sparrow Nest," which is usually described by *The Wiregrass Farmer,* our local paper, as "The Showplace of Turner County." The house was built in 1888 and the Victorian opulence is still intact. The old house has stained-glass windows, hanging Tiffany lamps in each room, china cabinets filled with antique silver that was buried during the War Between the States to keep it from being destroyed. The original furniture, paintings and tapestries are as they were during my childhood.

Grandmother Shingler, when she supervised the "Sparrow

Nest" kitchen, could be described as both a plain and fancy cook. By that I mean she would have the best liver pudding or souse meat at one meal, but if she wanted to have a light ladies' luncheon she would produce her Little Lemon Pies or other fancy foods.

DESSERT RECIPES
(Deliver me from these!)

CAKES
1-2-3-4 Cake
Applesauce Cake
Aunt Louise Cannon's
   Old-Fashioned Lane Cake
   Filling and Icing
Fresh Apple Cake
Carrot Cake
Cocoa Fudge Cake
Cornmeal Pound Cake
Country Pound Cake
Nutty Fruitcake
Lemon "Cheese" Cake
   Filling and Icing
Lemon Squares
"Plum Easy" Cake
Prune Cake
Southern Jam Cake
Mocha Fluff Frosting

PIES
Chess Pie
Little Lemon Pies
Macaroon Pie
Pecan Pie
Pecan Meringue Pie
Old-Fashioned Dried Peach Pie

COOKIES
Corn Flake Cookies
Ice Cream Wafers
Oatmeal Cookies
Ruby Wimberly's Pecan Sandies
Peanut Macaroons
Pecan Confections

OTHER DESSERTS
Boiled Custard
Peach County, Georgia, Cobbler
Brandied Peaches
Caramel Orange Slices
Coffee Coronet
Cranberry Ice Cream Dessert
Cup Custard
Aunt Lelia's Hot Fudge Sauce
Icebox Pudding
Lemon Bisque
Lemon Curd
Overnight Meringues
Peanut Butter Squares
Rosalynn Carter's Peanut Brittle
Spiced Pecans
Persimmon Pudding
Squire Pudding
Date-Nut Squares
Waffle "Turtles"

CAKES

1-2-3-4 Cake

1 cup butter
2 cups sugar
3 cups flour
4 eggs, separated

1 cup milk
1 teaspoon baking soda
2 teaspoons cream of tartar
1 teaspoon vanilla

Cream butter and sugar well. Add egg yolks and milk, then flour, soda and cream of tartar. Beat egg whites; add vanilla. Fold beaten whites into batter. Pour into well-greased bundt or tube pan. Bake at 350° F. for 45 minutes.

Applesauce Cake

1 cup sugar
½ cup butter
1½ teaspoons cocoa
2 cups flour
1 teaspoon cinnamon

¼ teaspoon cloves
1 cup chopped raisins
1 cup chopped walnuts
1 cup applesauce
2 teaspoons baking soda

Cream sugar and butter well. Mix cocoa, flour, cinnamon, cloves, raisins, walnuts and ½ cup applesauce. Add to butter-and-sugar mixture. Dissolve soda in the rest of the applesauce and add to mixture. Pour into well-greased bundt or layer-cake pan. Bake at 350° F. for 45 minutes.

Aunt Louise Cannon's
Old-Fashioned Lane Cake

*Men are especially fond of this cake. I guess it is because of
the wine or bourbon in the filling.*

8 eggs, separated
1 cup butter
2 cups sugar
4 cups flour
2 heaping teaspoons baking
    powder

pinch of salt
1 cup milk
1 teaspoon vanilla

Beat egg whites until stiff and set aside. Combine butter, sugar, flour,
baking powder and salt, and gradually add milk. Add vanilla. Fold in
egg whites. Bake in 3 layers. Grease 3 9-inch cake pans and sprinkle
with flour. Pour cake batter into pans, filling them not more than 2/3
full. Bake in 350° F. preheated oven for 45 minutes. When cool, remove from pans and fill with the following:

FILLING
Beat the 8 yolks and add 1 cup sugar, 1 stick butter, 1 cup raisins, 1 cup
pecans, 2 ounces of wine or bourbon, and 1 teaspoon vanilla. Cook in
double boiler until thick. Spread this filling between the layers.

WHITE ICING
2 cups sugar
1/2 cup water
2 to 3 tablespoons white corn
    syrup

whites of 2 eggs

Combine sugar, water and corn syrup and cook until the mixture forms
a soft ball in cold water. Beat the egg whites stiff and add. Spread over
top and sides of cake while still warm.

Fresh Apple Cake

1 cup flour
1 teaspoon baking soda
½ teaspoon salt
¾ teaspoon cinnamon
¼ cup shortening

1 cup sugar
1 egg, beaten
2 cups chopped apples
1 cup coarsely chopped pecans

Sift together flour, baking soda, salt and cinnamon. Cream shortening and sugar, beating until fluffy. Add egg gradually, beating well. Stir in apples. Add dry ingredients gradually. Beat until smooth. Blend in nuts. Bake in lightly greased (bottom only) 8 × 8 × 2-inch pan in a 350° F. oven for 45 minutes. Cool in pan on cooling rack.

Carrot Cake

1¼ cups oil
1¾ cups sugar
4 eggs
2 cups flour
½ teaspoon salt
1¾ teaspoons baking powder

1½ teaspoons soda
1½ teaspoons nutmeg
2¼ teaspoons cinnamon
2 cups grated raw carrots
1 cup chopped pecans

Preheat oven to 350° F. Grease and flour 3 8-inch layer-cake pans. Mix oil and sugar in large bowl. Beat in eggs, one at a time. Sift together dry ingredients and add to egg mixture, blending well. Stir in grated carrots and add pecans. Turn into prepared cake pans. Bake at 350° F. for 30 minutes. Cool in pans for 10 minutes. Prepare a simple frosting with pecan halves or carrot shavings for garnish if desired.

Cocoa Fudge Cake

This recipe is easy, especially when you follow the steps in this order:
1. In a saucepan, combine and bring to a rolling boil:

½ cup butter or margarine
½ cup shortening

4 tablespoons cocoa
1 cup water

2. Sift together into a bowl:

2 cups sugar   *2 cups sifted cake or all-purpose flour*

3. Pour cocoa mixture over sugar-and-flour mixture.
4. Add ½ cup buttermilk mixed with 1 teaspoon baking soda.
5. Add:

½ teaspoon salt   *3 eggs, beaten lightly*
½ teaspoon vanilla

Pour batter into a 15 × 10 × 1-inch greased floured pan (a cookie tin with raised edge is fine).
Bake at 325° F. for 30 minutes.

COCOA FROSTING
1. Bring to a boil, stirring constantly:

½ cup butter   *6 tablespoons milk*
4 tablespoons cocoa

2. Remove from heat. Pour 1 pound powdered sugar over.
3. Add 1 teaspoon vanilla.
4. Add 1 cup pecans, chopped (optional); mix well.
5. Spread on *warm* cake; when cool, cut into 20 pieces.

Country Pound Cake

I borrowed this recipe from Atlanta's #1 soul food cook, Deacon Lendell Burton, who bakes a half-dozen of them every morning to serve to his luncheon customers.

1 pound butter   *1 pound all-purpose flour*
1 pound sugar   *2 teaspoons lemon extract*
8 large eggs

Cream butter and sugar. Beat in eggs one by one. Add flour slowly. Add lemon extract. Pour batter into a tube or bundt pan and bake in a preheated 325° F. oven for 1 hour and 20 minutes, or until a toothpick or cake tester comes out dry.

Cornmeal Pound Cake

I feel sure one of Aunt Lillie's forebears handed down this recipe. It is strictly Charleston, South Carolina, where, I understand, it is called Indian Pound Cake. The recipe, handwritten in one of our family cookbooks, is as follows:

"Half pound of butter; the weight of eight eggs in sugar and the weight of six eggs in sifted cornmeal; eight eggs and a nutmeg or a teaspoon of cinnamon. Rub the butter and sugar to a cream; beat the eggs very lightly and stir them alternately with the meal into the butter and sugar. Add the spice and bake."

I have translated it into measurements we use today (I had to weigh the eggs on my mail scale) and came up with this version:

½ pound butter	2 cups cornmeal
2 cups sugar	1 teaspoon cinnamon
8 eggs, beaten	

Cream butter and sugar. Beat eggs lightly and stir them into creamed mixture alternately with the meal. Add cinnamon. Beat vigorously. Pour into tube pan. Cut into batter with knife to puncture air holes. Bake at 350° F. for at least 1½ hours.

Nutty Fruitcake

1¾ cups flour	1 pound dates, chopped
½ pound butter	1 pound crystallized pineapple, chopped
1 cup sugar	
½ teaspoon baking powder	4 cups chopped pecans
5 eggs, yolks and whites beaten separately	3 tablespoons vanilla
	3 tablespoons lemon extract
1 pound crystallized red cherries, chopped	

Use some of the flour to dredge fruit before chopping. Cream butter and sugar. Add flour, baking powder and egg yolks and whites. Add remaining ingredients. Line a tube pan with greased brown paper. Pour batter into tube pan and place in *cold* oven. Set oven at 300° F. and bake for 30 minutes, then lower to 250° F. and bake for 2½ hours more. Cool on cake rack.

Lemon "Cheese" Cake

1 cup butter
2 cups sugar
3 cups sifted flour
2 teaspoons baking powder

1 cup milk
1½ teaspoons vanilla
8 egg whites

Cream together butter and sugar. Sift flour and baking powder. Add to butter-and-sugar mixture alternately with milk and vanilla. Beat well. Beat egg whites and fold in. Bake in 3 8-inch or 9-inch pans, floured and greased. Put into cold oven, turn heat to 325° F. and bake for 30 to 35 minutes. Cool in pans for 10 minutes.

LEMON "CHEESE" FILLING

6 eggs, well beaten
2 cups sugar

¼ cup butter
½ cup lemon juice

Mix eggs, sugar, butter in top of double boiler. Add lemon juice. Cook until thick. Spread between layers. Secure layers with toothpicks.

ICING

2½ cups sugar
⅛ teaspoon salt
⅓ cup dark corn syrup

⅔ cup water
2 egg whites
1½ teaspoons vanilla

Dissolve sugar, salt and syrup in water. Put to boil and beat egg whites to foamy. When syrup boils, pour 3 tablespoons syrup over whites and set aside. Put the rest of the syrup back on fire until it spins a 10-inch thread. Pour this very, very gradually over whites-and-syrup mixture. Beat, add vanilla. Spread over top and sides of cake.

Lemon Squares

1 cup sifted flour   *½ cup melted butter*
¼ cup powdered sugar

Mix and press in 8-inch-square pan. Bake at 350° F. for 20 minutes. Then mix:

2 beaten eggs   *1 cup granulated sugar*
3 generous tablespoons lemon   *½ teaspoon baking powder*
   juice   *2 tablespoons flour*

Pour on top of first mixture. Return to oven for 25 minutes.

Cut into small squares (they're rich) and sprinkle with powdered sugar while still hot.

"Plum Easy" Cake

2 cups self-rising flour   *1 cup oil*
2 cups sugar   *2 small jars of plum with tapioca*
1 teaspoon cinnamon   *baby food*
1 teaspoon cloves   *1 cup chopped nuts*
3 eggs

Mix all ingredients. Bake at 325° F. for 75 minutes in bundt pan.

Prune Cake

1 cup sugar   *1½ cups flour*
½ cup butter   *1 teaspoon baking soda*
1 cup pitted and chopped   *½ teaspoon allspice*
   cooked prunes   *½ teaspoon cinnamon*
3 tablespoons sour cream   *½ teaspoon nutmeg*
3 eggs, separated

Cream sugar and butter well. Combine prunes with sour cream. Beat egg yolks until frothy. Add to prune-sour cream mixture. Blend in sugar-and-butter mixture. Combine flour, soda, allspice, cinnamon and nutmeg. Blend with other mixture. Beat egg whites until they stand in a peak. Fold into batter. Bake in bundt pan at 350° F. for 45 minutes.

Southern Jam Cake

¾ *cup butter*
½ *cup sugar*
1 *cup thick strawberry jam*
3 *eggs, separated*
2½ *cups sifted flour*
1 *teaspoon cinnamon*

¼ *teaspoon cloves*
½ *teaspoon salt*
½ *cup strong cold coffee*
1 *teaspoon vanilla*
1 *tablespoon baking soda*
4 *tablespoons sour cream*

Cream and beat butter and sugar until light and fluffy. Add jam. Mix well. Beat egg yolks until frothy, then add to mixture. Sift and measure flour, then sift again with spices and salt. Add sifted dry ingredients to creamed mixture alternately with the combined coffee and vanilla, stirring in the soda and sour cream just before adding the last batch of dry ingredients. Fold in the stiffly beaten egg whites. Turn into well-greased 9″ square cake pan. Bake at 350° F. for 40 to 45 minutes. Place on cake rack to cool. Remove from pan and frost.

MOCHA FLUFF FROSTING

1½ *cups light-brown sugar*
2 *egg whites*
   pinch of salt

1 *teaspoon vanilla flavoring*
5 *tablespoons cold strong coffee*

Combine all in top of double boiler. Stir well. Place over boiling water. Being careful not to allow the top of double boiler to touch the water, beat 5 to 7 minutes, until frosting stands in peaks. Remove from heat and continue beating until the frosting is slightly cooled. Cover cake with frosting.

PIES

Chess Pie

½ cup butter
1¼ cups sugar
4 egg yolks, well beaten
⅓ cup milk

½ cup sifted white cornmeal
grated fresh nutmeg (if not
   available, use 2 teaspoons
   vanilla)

Cream butter and sugar. Add egg yolks, milk, cornmeal and a small amount of nutmeg. Pour into an unbaked pastry shell and bake in a 325° F. oven for 45 minutes. Use this recipe for tarts, too.

Little Lemon Pies

6 eggs
2 cups sugar
2 tablespoons flour
2 tablespoons milk
   juice of 2 lemons, or more to
      taste (sometimes I add juice
      of 1 lime)

2 tablespoons butter
whipped cream

Beats eggs; combine sugar and flour and add to eggs. Beat thoroughly. Add milk. Cook in double boiler; add lemon juice and butter. Cook until butter melts and mixture has thickened. Pour into 12 little baked pie shells. Cool. Top with whipped cream and serve.

Macaroon Pie

⅜ cup soda cracker crumbs
2 ounces dates
⅝ cup sugar
⅜ cup pecans

¼ cup egg whites beaten to peak
   only (not too stiff)
¾ tablespoon almond flavoring

Crush crackers into crumbs. Cut dates into small pieces. Roll dates in crumbs. Add sugar, pecans, egg whites, almond flavoring. Press into pie tin. Bake at 325° F. for 30 minutes.

Pecan Pie

1 cup light corn syrup
2 eggs, beaten
2 tablespoons margarine

½ cup sugar
2 tablespoons flour
1 cup pecans

Mix all ingredients together and pour into an unbaked pastry shell. Bake at 325° F. until firm and shell is golden brown.

Pecan Meringue Pie

Quick, easy and delicious—a good way to use those good Georgia pecans!

3 egg whites
1 teaspoon baking powder
1 scant cup sugar
1 cup chopped pecans

20 crackers (Escort or Ritz type),
*   crushed*
1 teaspoon vanilla

Beat whites to froth; add baking powder and sugar and beat stiff. Fold in pecans, crushed crackers and vanilla. Pour into 9-inch pie pan. Bake for 30 minutes at 350° F.

Old-Fashioned Dried Peach Pie

2 cups cooked dried peaches,
*   sweetened to taste*
4 eggs, separated
9 tablespoons sugar

2 cups milk
2 teaspoons vanilla
*   baking powder (pinch)*

Line pie pan with pastry. Pour in cooked peaches. Beat together until light the egg yolks, 4 tablespoons sugar, milk and vanilla and pour over peaches. Place in oven to bake at 450° F. until crust browns. Then lower heat until done.

Beat egg whites with 5 tablespoons sugar and a pinch of baking powder until it holds a peak. Pour over baked custard and return to slow oven (300° F.) to brown.

COOKIES

Corn Flake Cookies

2 egg whites beaten very stiff
1 cup sugar
1 cup pecans, chopped fine

1 teaspoon vanilla or almond
*   flavoring*
3 cups corn flakes

Add the sugar to the egg whites. Mix in the rest of the ingredients. Drop by teaspoonfuls on buttered cookie sheet. Bake in a slow oven (300° F.) for 20 minutes. Yield: 2 dozen.

Ice Cream Wafers

½ cup sugar
½ cup butter
1 egg
¾ cup flour
½ teaspoon salt

½ teaspoon vanilla or almond
*   flavoring*
½ pecan or walnut for top of
*   each cookie*

Mix all ingredients. Drop by teaspoonfuls on buttered cookie sheet. Bake at 300° F. for 20 minutes. Yield: 2 dozen.

Oatmeal Cookies

1¼ sticks butter
2 cups sugar
2 eggs

1 teaspoon salt
2 teaspoons baking powder
2½ cups regular oatmeal

1 cup seedless raisins
2 teaspoons allspice
2 teaspoons cinnamon

1 cup nuts
1½ cups flour

Mix butter and sugar together; then mix in eggs, salt, baking powder, oatmeal, raisins, allspice, cinnamon and nuts. Now add enough flour to make a very stiff batter—sometimes not all the flour is needed. Grease a baking sheet and, using a fork and a spoon, place on it pieces about as large as a walnut, leaving plenty of room so the cookies will not touch during the baking. Bake in moderate oven (375° F.) 10 to 15 minutes. Yield: 5 dozen.

Ruby Wimberly's Pecan Sandies

1 cup butter (2 sticks or ½ pound)
4 tablespoons sugar
1 teaspoon vanilla

1 teaspoon ice water
2 cups all-purpose flour
1 cup finely chopped pecans
powdered sugar

Cream together well the butter and sugar. Add vanilla and ice water. Mix in the flour, a little at a time. Mix in the pecans. Roll into tiny balls and bake on an ungreased sheet in a 300° F. oven for 30 minutes or until slightly brown. When cooled to just warm, roll in powdered sugar, then roll again. Yield: 3 to 4 dozen.

Peanut Macaroons

¼ cup peanut butter
¼ cup egg whites (2 eggs)
pinch of salt

½ teaspoon vanilla
⅔ cup sugar
1⅓ cups shredded coconut

Melt peanut butter over low heat and cool slightly. Beat egg whites with salt and vanilla until they form soft peaks. Add sugar gradually, beating until peaks are stiff. Fold in coconut and melted peanut butter. Drop by teaspoonfuls onto greased cookie sheet and bake in 325° F. oven for 20 minutes. Cool at least 1 minute before removing to wire rack. Yield: 2 dozen.

Pecan Confections

This is the way the recipe is written in an old notebook I found in the kitchen. When I tried it recently, the cookies were just as delicious as I remembered:

"Beat 1 egg white to a stiff froth; add gradually 1 cupful of brown sugar, 1 pinch salt, 1 level tablespoon of flour. Stir in 1 cupful of chopped pecans, and drop by small spoonfuls on greased tins. Bake in slow oven (325° F.) for 15 minutes. Cool slightly before removing from tins." Yield: 2 dozen.

OTHER DESSERTS

Boiled Custard

2 cups milk
2 tablespoons sugar
1 tablespoon cornstarch

3 eggs
1 teaspoon vanilla

Heat milk. Combine sugar and cornstarch. Beat eggs and add sugar mixture. Gradually pour into scalding milk, stirring constantly. It is safer to use a double boiler than a pot directly over heat, so that the pudding will thicken without burning. Do not boil. When pudding thickens, add vanilla and remove from heat. Pour into individual dishes. Top with a dab of fruit or wine jelly. Chill. Serves 6.

Peach County, Georgia, Cobbler

This recipe is one you can use with apples, blackberries and blueberries.

Melt in large, shallow casserole 1 stick butter. Make a batter of 1 cup all-purpose flour, 1 cup sugar, ½ teaspoon salt, 3 teaspoons baking powder, scant cup of milk. Pour batter over butter in casserole. Do not stir. Place on top of batter 2 cups Georgia peaches, peeled, cut up and sweetened with 1 cup sugar. *Do not mix or stir.* Bake for 1 hour at 350° F. Serve hot or cold with milk, whipped cream or ice cream. Serves 8.

Brandied Peaches

4 tablespoons butter	*4 fresh peaches, peeled*
½ cup sugar	*3 ounces brandy*
¼ cup water	

Place butter and sugar in top of double boiler; cook over boiling water until melted. Stir in water; add peaches. Cook for 30 to 35 minutes, turning peaches several times. Add brandy; serve. Serves 4.

Caramel Orange Slices

Peel 4 navel oranges, removing membrane, and slice approximately ¼ inch thick. Cut the peel from one orange into thin strings and boil in water to cover for 10 minutes. Drain. Sprinkle rind over orange slices. Caramelize 1 cup sugar in this manner: In a heavy pan, boil 1 cup sugar with ¼ cup water. Boil until it turns a golden color. Do not stir but, if necessary, shake pan gently. Cool for 5 minutes. Sprinkle slices with 3 to 4 tablespoons orange liqueur and dribble caramel over them. Chill. Serve the same day or the crusty caramel will melt. Serves 6.

Coffee Coronet

2 envelopes unflavored gelatin
½ cup strong cold coffee
½ cup strong hot coffee
1 cup sugar plus 3 teaspoons
2 dozen ladyfingers (about)
½ package (3 ounces) semisweet
   chocolate pieces, melted

2 cups heavy cream
1 tablespoon rum flavoring
1 cup broken pecans
1 teaspoon finely ground coffee

Sprinkle gelatin on cold coffee. Add hot coffee and the cup of sugar and stir until dissolved. Chill until mixture has consistency of unbeaten egg whites.

Meanwhile split 9 or 10 ladyfingers and dip one end of each into melted chocolate. Whip chilled gelatin mixture until light and fluffy. Whip cream and fold in with rum flavoring and pecans. Spoon into spring-form pan to a depth of about ½ inch. Stand chocolate-tipped ladyfingers upright around edge of pan, chocolate tips upmost. Add about ⅓ gelatin mixture and layer with plain split ladyfingers. Add another third of gelatin mixture, another layer of split ladyfingers and a top layer of gelatin. Chill until firm. Just before serving, sprinkle with a mixture of 3 teaspoons sugar and 1 teaspoon very finely ground coffee. Garnish with additional whipped cream and sugar-coffee mixture. Unmold to serve. Serves 12.

Cranberry Ice Cream Dessert

1 cup cranberry juice cocktail
1 3-ounce package raspberry
   gelatin
   dash of salt

1 cup slightly softened vanilla
   ice cream
¼ to ½ banana

Heat ½ cup cranberry juice cocktail to boiling. Pour into blender with gelatin and salt. Process on low speed until gelatin is dissolved. Blend in rest of cranberry juice, ice cream and banana with blender on low speed. Process until ice cream and banana are liquefied and mixture is light and fluffy (about 1 minute). Pour into mold (or small individual molds) and refrigerate 1 to 2 hours, or until firm. Unmold to serve. Serves 6.

Cup Custard

2 *cups milk*
3 *eggs*
¼ *cup sugar*

⅛ *teaspoon salt*
¾ *teaspoon vanilla extract*
    nutmeg

Scald milk; beat eggs. Mix sugar and salt with milk and pour slowly over the eggs. Add the vanilla extract. Sprinkle nutmeg on top. Beat custard until well blended. Pour into 4 greased custard cups. Set cups in pan of hot water. Bake at 325° F. for 45 minutes. Test with knife. Custard is done when knife comes out clean. Serves 4.

Aunt Lelia's Hot Fudge Sauce

3 *tablespoons cocoa or 1½*
    squares semisweet chocolate
¾ *cup dark-brown sugar*
¾ *cup granulated sugar*
    dash of salt

1 *cup milk or half milk, half*
    water
1 *tablespoon butter*
½ *teaspoon vanilla*

Combine cocoa or chocolate, sugars and salt; add milk (or milk and water) and place over low flame. Stir constantly until sugar dissolves and mixture is boiling. Add butter and vanilla. Continue cooking without stirring until a candy thermometer reaches 220° F. or until a small amount dropped into cold water forms a jellied mass. Remove from heat and serve over ice cream or cake.

Icebox Pudding

8 ounces vanilla wafers
2 eggs, separated
½ cup sugar
½ cup pecans

½ cup melted butter
pinch salt
1 small can crushed pineapple

Crush wafers. Add egg yolks, sugar, pecans, butter, salt, pineapple and mix well. Last, fold in well-beaten egg whites. Chill in refrigerator for 24 hours. Serve with whipped cream and cherries. Serves 8.

Lemon Bisque

1 large can evaporated milk
1¼ cups boiling water
1 package lemon gelatin
¾ cup sugar

juice of 2 lemons
grated rind of 1 lemon
1 cup graham cracker crumbs

Place evaporated milk in refrigerator overnight to chill thoroughly. Pour boiling water over gelatin. Add sugar, lemon juice and rind. Stir until dissolved. Let set until it begins to jell; then fold in the milk, which has been whipped stiff. Line an attractive serving dish with graham cracker crumbs; pour mixture over; add enough cracker crumbs to cover top. Chill and serve with whipped cream, cherries, etc.

Lemon Curd

1 cup sugar
3 large lemons (juice and rind)

5 eggs
1 stick butter

Mix sugar, lemon juice and lemon rind and eggs in blender. Melt butter in double boiler. Add melted butter to other ingredients in blender. Blend. Pour into double boiler and cook 4 to 5 minutes. Excellent served on toasted pound cake.

Overnight Meringues

6 egg whites (¾ cup)   2 cups sugar
½ teaspoon cream of tartar

Heat oven to 400° F. Beat egg whites with cream of tartar until frothy.
Beat in sugar a little at a time; continue to beat until stiff and glossy.
Drop by small spoonfuls on brown paper on baking sheet, or heap into
high mounds and hollow out with back of spoon. Put into oven. Close
door. Turn off oven. Let stand overnight in oven. Don't peek!

Peanut Butter Squares

1 cup butter   1 package (12 ounces) chocolate
1 cup peanut butter   chips
1 box powdered sugar (1 pound)
1 package graham crackers
   (crush to crumbs)

Mix all ingredients except chocolate chips. Press into 9 × 13-inch pan
lined with foil. Melt chocolate chips and spread on top. Refrigerate for
about 30 minutes. Then score chocolate so that it won't break when
cutting into *small* pieces. These are very rich but very good. Return to
refrigerator to set completely. Yield: 54 1½″ squares.

Rosalynn Carter's Peanut Brittle

3 cups sugar   2 tablespoons baking soda
1½ cups water   ½ stick butter
1 cup white corn syrup   1 teaspoon vanilla
3 cups raw peanuts

Boil sugar, water and syrup until it spins a thread; add peanuts. After
adding peanuts, stir constantly until syrup turns golden brown. Remove from heat. Add remaining ingredients; stir until butter melts.

Pour quickly onto 2 cookie sheets with sides. As mixture begins to harden around edges, pull until thin. When cool, break into pieces.

Spiced Pecans

½ *cup sugar*	¼ *teaspoon nutmeg*
¾ *teaspoon salt*	*1 egg white*
1 teaspoon cinnamon	*2 tablespoons water*
¼ *teaspoon ground cloves*	*2 cups pecans*

Mix sugar, salt, cinnamon, cloves and nutmeg. Beat the egg white with the water until very thin. Stir in the pecans. Sprinkle spice mixture over pecans. Mix thoroughly. Spread out on cookie sheet and bake at 300° F. for 30 minutes. Cool and dry on paper towels.

Persimmon Pudding

*1*½ *cups sifted flour*	½ *cup chopped dates*
1 cup sugar	½ *cup raisins*
½ *teaspoon salt*	*1 cup soft bread crumbs*
*1*½ *teaspoons baking powder*	*1 cup chopped pecans*
*1*½ *teaspoons baking soda*	*1*½ *teaspoons butter*
1 cup persimmon pulp	½ *cup milk*

Resift flour with sugar, salt, baking powder and soda. Add other ingredients and mix thoroughly. Grease 9 × 5 × 3-inch loaf pan and line with wax paper. Add mixture to pan and bake at 350° F. for about 1½ hours or until center is firm. Serve with whipped cream if desired.

Date-Nut Squares

3 egg whites	*12 dates*
¾ *cup sugar*	¾ *cup nuts*
12 saltine crackers	½ *pint whipping cream*

Beat egg whites until frothy. Add sugar. Crush crackers very fine. Combine dates and nuts with crackers. Add to egg whites.

Bake at 325° F. for 30 minutes in an 8½-inch-square pan. Slice in squares, top with whipped cream. Yield: 16 2″ squares.

Squire Pudding

Bake a 3-layer cake, using one of your own favorite recipes. While the cake is baking make this "Tipsy Custard":

1 quart milk	*1 pint whipping cream*
4 eggs	*½ cup wine*
1½ cups sugar	*¼ pound chopped pecans*
4 tablespoons flour	

First, heat milk in double boiler. In a bowl, beat eggs and add sugar and flour. Add this mixture to hot milk and stir well. This should cook until thick. Do not boil.

While custard is cooking, whip the cream. Place 1 layer of cake in bottom of deep pan, pour ⅓ the wine over it; spread ⅓ of the custard mixture over that and sprinkle with ⅓ the chopped nuts. Top this with ⅓ of the whipped cream. Cover with another layer, topped the same way. Stack and top the 3rd layer. Let stand long enough for the flavoring to soak well into the cake.

Waffle "Turtles"

Louise Hastings and I share similar childhood memories of having chocolate waffles for Sunday-night supper. Instead of having waffles and syrup as a main supper dish, we would make miniature waffles for dessert, topping each one with a dab of cake frosting and a pecan half. They looked like candy turtles.

2 squares (1 ounce) semisweet chocolate	*¾ cup sugar*
⅓ cup butter or margarine	*1 teaspoon vanilla*
2 eggs, beaten	*1 cup all-purpose flour*
	pecans

In a heavy saucepan, melt chocolate and butter, stirring constantly. Cool. Combine eggs, sugar and vanilla with the chocolate mixture. Add flour and mix well. Preheat waffle iron. Drop batter by teaspoonfuls 2 inches apart. Close waffle iron and bake about 2 minutes or until they are done. Cool on rack and frost as desired. Top each with a pecan. Yield: 2 dozen.

HOT BREADS

Hot breads were on the table at every meal while I was growing up—no doubt the reason I've spent some painful periods of my life shedding pounds.

For some reason, baking a loaf of bread gives me a great sense of achievement. Eating it gives me a strong sense of guilt, along with a great deal of pleasure. There are many different recipes for the best of the hot breads—and when they call for butter, margarine can be used with equally good results.

BREAD RECIPES

Banana Bread
Buckwheat Cakes
Syrup
Buttermilk-Sweet Potato Biscuits
Buttermilk Brown Bread with
　Raisins
Coffee Can Sweet Bread
Coffee Can Whole Wheat Bread
Coffee Can Health Bread
Corn Sticks
'Cile's Cracklin' Corn Pones
Buttermilk Corn Bread

'Cile's Cracklin' Bread
Cranberry Bread
Hoecakes
Spicy Hot Corn Bread
Hush Puppies #1 and #2
Hot Sally Lunn Bread
Johnnie Cake
Lace-edged Corn Cakes
Spoon Bread #1 and #2
Waffles and Orange Syrup
Aunt Louisa's Yeast Rolls

Banana Bread

½ cup shortening
1 cup sugar
2 eggs
1 cup mashed overripe bananas
1 teaspoon lemon juice

2 cups flour
3 teaspoons baking powder
½ teaspoon salt
1 cup chopped nuts

Cream shortening and sugar together. Beat eggs until light and add. Press bananas through sieve and add lemon juice. Combine with creamed mixture. Sift flour, salt and baking powder together. Add nuts. Bake in greased loaf pan in moderate oven at 375° F. for 1¼ hours. Makes a 1-pound loaf.

Buckwheat Cakes

1 cup buckwheat flour
½ cup plain flour
3 teaspoons baking powder
¾ teaspoon salt

2 teaspoons molasses
1 tablespoon melted butter
1¼ cups milk

Sift dry ingredients; add molasses and butter to milk. Combine ingredients and beat well. Bake on a lightly buttered hot griddle, turning once. Yield: 14 cakes.

SYRUP

If you run out of molasses or cane syrup for your pancakes, make your own this way:

1 cup white sugar
¼ cup water

1 teaspoon butter or margarine
1 teaspoon vanilla

Boil sugar and water at least 5 minutes after boiling begins. Take off fire and add butter and vanilla. Yield: 1 cup.

Buttermilk-Sweet Potato Biscuits

5 tablespoons butter
2½ cups all-purpose flour
1 cup mashed cold dry sweet
  potatoes
1 teaspoon salt
1 tablespoon sugar

2 teaspoons baking soda
½ teaspoon double-acting baking
  powder
¼ teaspoon grated orange rind
1 cup (scant) buttermilk

Cut *cold* butter into flour; add *cold* mashed sweet potatoes by cutting in the same way; add salt, sugar, baking soda, baking powder and orange rind; toss well.

Next add the buttermilk; mix quickly by hand. Roll lightly or pat on floured board.

Cut with biscuit cutter. Brush tops with melted butter. Bake in 400° F. oven for 12 minutes. Makes 20 to 26.

Buttermilk Brown Bread with Raisins

2 cups whole wheat flour
1 cup buttermilk
½ cup molasses
2 tablespoons sugar
¼ teaspoon salt

1 teaspoon baking soda
2 tablespoons hot water
1¼ cups seedless (or seeded
  muscat) raisins

Mix whole wheat flour with buttermilk, molasses, sugar, salt and baking soda mixed with hot water. Fold in raisins. Pour batter into greased 9 × 5 × 3-inch bread pan lined with buttered wax paper. Bake at 350° F. (moderate oven) for about 50 minutes. Cool on wire rack. Yield: 1 loaf.

If you want to make two loaves at a time and freeze one, double the recipe.

Coffee Can Sweet Bread

1 package dry yeast
2 cups warm milk (make with dry milk powder if you wish)
2 cups very warm water
½ cup sugar or honey
1 cup cooking oil (preferably safflower oil)
8 cups white flour (preferably unbleached)
1 tablespoon salt

2 eggs, lightly beaten
2 cups raisins
1 tablespoon dried or fresh lemon peel
1 tablespoon cardamom (optional)
1 tablespoon vanilla extract
4 or 5 1-pound coffee cans, well oiled

Dissolve yeast in milk and water; add sugar or honey and oil. Beat in 3 cups of flour and let stand until batter forms bubbles; then add the salt and all other ingredients with the remaining flour. Knead well, let stand covered in warm place until double in bulk. Turn out on floured counter and knead again. Return to oiled bowl, brush top with oil and let rise again. Knead until smooth, and divide into the well-oiled cans. Brush tops of dough with oil. Let stand for 5 to 10 minutes. Start in cold oven on bottom rack at 350° F. Bake until tester comes out clean, 35 to 45 minutes. Let cool in can for no more than 5 minutes. Slide out on wire rack and cool. May be refrigerated.

If you feel that the dough is stiff enough at second kneading, just oil your counter top and knead on oil instead of adding more flour to keep from sticking. (Use cans for baking no more than twice.) Makes 4 to 5 loaves.

Option: Roll dough to 2-inch thickness, brush with melted butter or margarine, sprinkle with generous amount of cinnamon, roll and divide to fill coffee cans ¾ full.

Coffee Can Whole Wheat Bread

1½ cups vegetable oil
2 cups milk (use powdered
   milk combined with warm
   water to make 2 cups if you
   wish)
1½ packages dry yeast
4 tablespoons sugar

4 to 5 cups unbleached white
   flour
1½ tablespoons salt
4 to 5 cups whole wheat flour
4 or 5 1-pound coffee cans, very
   well oiled

Mix together oil, milk, yeast and sugar. Beat in with mixer or by hand 4 to 5 cups unbleached white flour. Let stand until batter forms bubbles.

Add salt and as much whole wheat flour as dough will hold. You may use only 3 cups white flour and more whole wheat, if you wish. Knead dough very well; kneading is most important for good texture and taste. Cover with oil, return to oiled bowl and let rise until double in size. Punch down and knead again. Let rise again. The second rising will take less time. Punch down again and knead until smooth. Divide into equal parts and fill coffee cans ¾ full. Brush tops with oil and let rise for 5 minutes.

Place in cold oven on bottom rack at 350° F. and bake for about 40 to 45 minutes. Insert cake tester—if no dough sticks to tester, bread is done. Let cool on a wire rack for *no more than 10 minutes* (bread gets soggy), slide out and finish cooling. The loaves freeze well. Makes 4 to 5 loaves.

Coffee Can Health Bread

2 packages dry yeast or 1 cake
   fresh yeast (1½ ounces)
3 cups very warm milk (powdered milk may be used)
1½ cups safflower oil
4 tablespoons honey (raw
   honey, if possible)

⅔ cup soy flour
4 to 5 cups whole wheat flour
4 to 5 cups unbleached white
   flour
1½ tablespoons sea salt
⅔ cup raw bran
⅔ cup raw wheat germ

⅔ cup unsweetened shredded coconut flakes 1½ cups unsalted sunflower seeds

Dissolve yeast in milk; add oil, honey and as much flour as liquid will absorb; mix well and let sit until bubbly, about 10 to 15 minutes. Add salt and remaining ingredients, first beating in with wooden spoon and later kneading the dough until smooth. Let dough rise, brush with oil and put in warm place until double in size. Punch down and knead. Let it rise again. The second rising will take less time. Knead again until smooth and divide into equal parts and fill well-oiled 1-pound coffee cans ¾ full. Let rise again or start in cold oven on bottom rack at 350° F. Bake for about 40 to 50 minutes. Insert cake tester; if tester comes out clean, bread is done. Leave in cans to cool for only 10 minutes. (Bread becomes soggy if left in can.) Finish cooling on wire rack. Coffee cans can only be used twice or the bread will stick to the cans. Bread can also be baked in 3-pound cans or regular loaf pans. Increase baking time for 3-pound cans. Makes 2 3-pound coffee cans or 5 1-pound loaf pans.

Corn Sticks

2 cups cornmeal
2 tablespoons flour
2 teaspoons baking powder
1 teaspoon salt

1 egg, beaten
1⅔ cup milk
¼ cup bacon drippings

Grease 2 iron corn stick pans and place in 450° F. oven to heat while batter is being mixed. Sift cornmeal, flour, baking powder and salt together. Mix egg and milk and blend into dry ingredients. Pour in the bacon drippings. Pour into the pans, which should be very hot. Bake for 15 or 20 minutes. Serve immediately.

If you wish to use a regular muffin pan, reduce temperature to 400° F. and bake for 30 minutes or until done. Yield: 12 corn sticks or muffins.

'Cile's Cracklin' Corn Pones

*1½ cups self-rising cornmeal (if
     you use plain meal, add 1
     teaspoon salt)*
*1 cup water (or, as 'Cile says,
     "Just enough to make it stick
     together")*

*1 cup cracklin's (be sure they are
     fresh)*

Mix all ingredients together and pinch off enough to roll in hand to form individual oblong small pones. Place on baking sheet. First brown under the broiler and then place in oven to bake 10 to 15 minutes at 300° F.

Buttermilk Corn Bread

1 teaspoon baking soda
¼ teaspoon baking powder
1 teaspoon salt
*¼ cup sugar (or 3 tablespoons
     honey)*
2 cups buttermilk

*2 cups cornmeal, yellow or white
     (water-ground white is best
     but hard to find)*
½ cup flour
6 tablespoons shortening, melted

Preheat oven to 400° F. Combine baking soda, baking powder, salt and sugar or honey. Stir in buttermilk. Add cornmeal and flour alternately. Add melted shortening and stir until smooth. Grease pan well. Pour mixture into 8½ × 8½-inch baking pan or muffin tins and bake for 30 to 40 minutes. Cut into individual squares if baked in baking pan. Yield: 9 squares or 12 muffins.

'Cile's Cracklin' Bread

1½ cups cornmeal
1 teaspoon salt
1 teaspoon baking powder

1 cup cracklin's
1 egg
1½ cups buttermilk

Mix dry ingredients together. Stir in cracklin's. Beat egg, add to buttermilk and combine with dry mixture. Grease a heavy skillet or shallow casserole, pour in batter and bake at 450° F. about 20 minutes, or until it springs back to the touch.

Cranberry Bread

¼ *cup butter*
1 *cup sugar*
1 *egg, well beaten*
2 *cups flour*
1½ *teaspoons baking powder*
1 *teaspoon salt*
½ *teaspoon baking soda*

1 *cup orange juice*
½ *cup chopped pecans*
½ *cup dried apricots, chopped*
1 *tablespoon grated orange rind*
2 *cups fresh cranberries, chopped (or frozen unsweetened cranberries)*

Cream butter and sugar. Add egg. Sift flour, baking powder, salt and soda together. Add flour mixture and orange juice alternately to sugar-and-egg mixture. Add pecans, apricots, orange rind, and fold in cranberries carefully. Spoon into greased loaf pan and bake for 1 hour at 350° F. Let cool overnight.

Hoecakes

1 *cup white water-ground corn-meal*
½ *teaspoon salt*

¾ *cup boiling water*
2 *tablespoons bacon drippings*

Combine cornmeal and salt. Slowly add water, stirring constantly. Beat until smooth. Heat bacon drippings in heavy griddle. Make hoecake batter into flat, round cakes. When fat is very hot, reduce heat to low. Add hoecakes and fry a few minutes on each side until brown. Yield: approximately 1 dozen.

Spicy Hot Corn Bread

2½ *cups cornmeal*
1 *cup flour*
2 *tablespoons sugar*
1 *tablespoon salt*
4 *teaspoons baking powder*
3 *eggs*
1½ *cups milk*
½ *cup vegetable oil*

1 *can (16 ounces) cream-style*
   corn
6 *small hot chili peppers, chopped*
   (canned or fresh)
2 *cups grated sharp Cheddar*
   cheese
2 *cups onion*

Stir together cornmeal, flour, sugar, salt and baking powder. In a separate bowl, beat eggs lightly and stir in milk and oil. Add liquid mixture to cornmeal mixture. Stir in the corn, hot peppers, cheese and onions. Pour batter into 2 well-oiled pans (9 × 11 inches) and bake at 425° F. for 35 minutes or until done. This bread is best served at room temperature and is excellent as finger food if cut into small squares. Serves 12.

Hush Puppies #1

A platter of these will stretch any fried-chicken buffet when you're not sure how many guests are coming or how much they will eat.

1 *cup plain cornmeal*
2 *teaspoons baking powder*
1 *teaspoon salt*
1 *tablespoon sugar*

1 *egg, beaten*
1 *onion, chopped or grated*
½ *cup (scant) milk*
   fat for deep frying

Mix all dry ingredients. Mix egg and onion with milk and gradually add to dry mixture until mixture is moist enough to drop by spoonfuls into deep fat. Fry until golden brown. Drain on paper towels. Yield: approximately 20.

Hush Puppies #2

1 cup plain cornmeal	*1 cup thick buttermilk*
½ cup flour	*¼ teaspoon baking soda*
1 teaspoon salt	*1 onion, chopped or grated*
1 teaspoon baking powder	*fat for deep frying*
1 egg	

Sift meal, flour, salt and baking powder together. Beat egg in buttermilk, add soda and combine with dry ingredients. Stir in chopped onion. Drop by teaspoonfuls into hot fat. Turn when brown. Drain on paper towels. Yield: approximately 20.

Hot Sally Lunn Bread

Some say this is the only authentic recipe, but there are so many variations that I refuse to take a stand. Here is one way it appears in my recipe file:

Scald ¾ cup of milk. Add 2 tablespoons sugar, 2 tablespoons butter. Cool to lukewarm. Add ½ cake fresh yeast, crumbled, or use ½ package of quick dry yeast and dissolve in ¼ cup lukewarm water; in that case reduce milk by ¼ cup. Stir until well blended. Add 2 eggs, beaten. Then add 2½ cups flour to make a soft dough. Put into a deep, greased bowl. When it doubles in size, punch dough down with a spoon. Pour into a well-greased round pan. Let double in bulk again. (It takes about an hour.) Bake in moderate oven (350° F.) about 30 to 40 minutes, greasing top with butter once or twice during baking. Serve hot.

Johnnie Cake

1 cup cornmeal	*1¼ cups boiling water*
1 tablespoon sugar	*½ cup milk*
1 tablespoon salt	*fat for frying*

Combine meal, sugar and salt. Blend in water until mixture is smooth. Add milk a little at a time. Drop with a spoon into hot fat. Fry slowly. Turn once. Yield: 10 cakes.

Lace-edged Corn Cakes

2 *eggs*
2 *cups milk*
1½ *cups cornmeal*

1 *teaspoon salt*
3 *tablespoons melted butter or*
   margarine

Beat eggs well and add milk while beating. Add cornmeal, salt and butter. Stir well each time you drop a spoonful of the batter on a well-greased hot griddle. The cakes will have a lacy edge. These are an attractive side dish with broiled or fried ham. Yield: 30 or 40 cakes.

Spoon Bread #1

2 *cups milk*
1 *cup cornmeal*
2 *eggs, separated*

1 *tablespoon butter*
1 *teaspoon salt*

Scald milk and add cornmeal. Add yolks, butter and salt. Continue to cook until smooth and thick. Remove from heat and stir in beaten whites. Bake in a well-greased casserole for 45 minutes at 350 °F. Serves 6.

Spoon Bread #2

2 *cups milk*
1 *teaspoon salt*
⅔ *cup cornmeal*
1 *tablespoon sugar*

2 *tablespoons butter or margarine*
3 *eggs*
2 *teaspoons baking powder*

In a saucepan, over gentle heat, make a stiff mush by stirring milk, salt, cornmeal, sugar and butter or margarine together. Remove from heat and continue to stir until slightly cooled. Stir in eggs and beat hard. Then add 2 teaspoons baking powder. Pour into greased casserole and bake in moderate oven (375° F.) for 30 to 40 minutes. Serve with plenty of butter or margarine. Serves 6.

Waffles

Waffles, served with ham or sausage, make an easy and economical luncheon. The Orange Syrup below turns them into a party dish.

2 cups flour
2 teaspoons baking powder
½ teaspoon salt
3 eggs, separated

1½ cups milk
4 tablespoons butter or
    margarine

Sift flour, baking powder and salt together. Add milk to yolks, beaten thick, and stir in dry ingredients, beating well. Add melted butter or margarine. Fold in lightly beaten whites. Bake in hot waffle iron. Yield: 8 waffles.

ORANGE SYRUP

This is especially good on waffles.

2 cups sugar
¾ cup orange juice

3 tablespoons white corn syrup
1 teaspoon grated orange rind

Combine sugar, orange juice, corn syrup and orange rind. Boil slowly for about 10 minutes or until syrup is thick. Yield: 2 cups.

Aunt Louisa's Yeast Rolls

1 package dry yeast
1 cup warm water
1 cup warm milk
2 tablespoons shortening

2 tablespoons sugar
2 teaspoons salt
5 to 6 cups flour

Dissolve yeast in warm water and milk and combine with shortening, sugar, and salt. Beat in flour, 1 cup at a time, until dough is stiff. Brush with oil and let rise in a warm place until double in size. Turn out on floured board and knead in as much flour as dough will absorb. Let rise for 15 minutes, punch down, knead until smooth. Roll out to 2-inch thickness. Cut with biscuit cutter and place on greased cookie sheet. Slash tops with sharp knife. Brush with water. Put in cold oven; turn heat to 375° F. and bake until rolls are light brown, approximately 20 minutes.

These rolls can be frozen and reheated. To reheat, brush rolls with cold water, put in 350° F. oven and bake for 10 minutes.

Pigs are coming into style. County fairs are being named for them in Georgia.

At Climax, Georgia, the community had the first Swine Time and it was a great success—Bluegrass music, played by the Country Grunts, and a hog-calling contest drew enthusiastic squeals from the pigs on display in nearby pens!

PART V

There's More to Pickle Than Pigs' Feet: Home Canning Recipes "From Here to Hahira"

NOT MANY PEOPLE outside of Georgia have ever heard the term "wiregrass country." Much of South Georgia is either farmland or pine trees, and the grass that grows wild under the pines is called wiregrass. The growth provides good feed for cattle, so farmers are grateful for nature's bounty.

My family's home in Ashburn is in Turner County. About seventy miles farther south is Lowndes County, where Lyniece Talmadge, my daughter-in-law, grew up on her parents' farm in Hahira.

"From here to Hahira" is an expression South Georgians use to describe the length of any journey when they don't know the exact distance. Perhaps it's another way of saying "From here to eternity." Lyniece's parents, Idella and Louie North, still live off the land in every sense of the term. The Norths grow, can, pickle or freeze almost all of the food the family eats, and Idella shares her home-prepared foods with friends and relatives. I have relied on her recipes through the years.

Lyniece learned to can and pickle in her mother's kitchen. She was once awarded a state prize for a high school 4-H Club project on methods of freezing fresh produce. She put into the home freezer 2,478 pounds of meat, 1,225 quarts of fruits and vegetables and 207 packages of prepared foods. Figuring the retail cost of food at the time, Lyniece said, she estimated she had saved $1,831 for the family. Imagine how much the savings would add up to today!

Although "Gold Leaf" tobacco is the main crop around Hahira, the Norths have a variety of produce. The family gathers apples from a small orchard, picks grapes, peaches, plums and black-berries. They have a vegetable garden too, so there is always something to can, pickle or freeze.

In 1964, one page of Lyniece's 4-H Senior Food Preparation Record includes this entry:

SPECIAL MEAL: *Number of times you planned and served a special meal for a party of at least eight:*
Grannie's Birthday Dinner for 50 guests—chicken, steak, ham, butterbeans, peas, rice, cheese & macaroni, corn bread, barbecue pork chops, tossed salad, green bean salad, varied sandwiches, iced tea, lemonade, cake and ice cream.

I always figured our son, Robert, must have read that page and decided to marry her then and there. She certainly fits into the Talmadge family!

Lyniece and Idella are my canning and pickling authorities.

If it is true—and the Gallup Poll says it's so—that more than 41 percent of all households in the United States have some kind of vegetable garden, I guess the rise of inflation brings about a rise of "green-thumbers."

Many will experience, for the first time, a sudden abundance of certain foods and will can or freeze the surplus. There are four excellent Bulletins* from the U.S. Department of Agriculture that novice home farmers should have on the shelf with their fancier cookbooks:

1. "Home Freezing of Fruits and Vegetables" (Home and Garden Bulletin No. 10)

* The Bulletins can be obtained for a nominal fee by writing the Superintendent of Documents, U.S. Government Printing Office, Washington, D.C. 20402.

2. "How to Make Jellies, Jams, and Preserves at Home" (Home and Garden Bulletin No. 56)

3. "Home Canning of Fruits and Vegetables" (Home and Garden Bulletin No. 8)

4. "Making Pickles and Relishes at Home" (Home and Garden Bulletin No. 92)

These booklets are clearly written, contain excellent instructions and recipes and are well illustrated. I can promise they'll save you time and tears.

They also go into all of the methods of canning and itemize the "do's and don'ts" of sterilizing, sealing and storing home-canned foods. I would recommend that a serious home canner study the procedures carefully.

I have tried to select recipes that are not too complicated and that require only enough produce to be canned and eaten within a reasonable time.

FREEZING, CANNING AND PICKLING RECIPES

Frozen Strawberries Packed in Sugar

Peaches Packed in Syrup

Figs

Frozen Tomatoes

Pepper Jelly

Indian Springs Pear Relish

Aunt Clyde's Mustard Pickles

Beet Pickles

Fresh Dill Pickles

9-Day Pickles

Green Tomato Pickles

Peach Pickles

Pear Honey

Fig Preserves

Quick and Easy Strawberry Figs

Idella's Watermelon Rind Preserves

Apple Jelly

Blackberry Jelly

Apple Butter

Applesauce

Tomato Ketchup

Vegetables for Soups

Idella North's Homemade Country Butter

1

Home Freezing
Fruits and Vegetables

FREEZING IS the best and easiest way of preserving fresh foods for home use. Remember, all freezing containers should be moisture-proof and airtight. You can use plastic freezer cartons, freezer jars and transparent plastic bags made for freezing. I suggest placing plastic bags inside freezer cartons until frozen. Then they can be removed and stacked. The cartons can be reused.

Frozen Strawberries Packed in Sugar

If you are buying strawberries rather than freezing homegrown ones, buy only in season and select firm, ripe strawberries—about ⅔ quart fresh berries are needed for each pint frozen. Wash berries a few at a time in cold water. Lift out gently and drain. Remove hulls; then slice berries into a bowl or shallow pan. Sprinkle sugar over berries—¾ cup to each quart (1⅓ pounds) berries. Turn berries over and over until sugar is dissolved and juice is formed.

Pack berries in containers, leaving ½-inch head space in the wide-mouthed pint box. Place a small piece of freezer paper or transparent polyethylene wrap on top of berries. Press berries down into juice. Press lid on firmly to seal. Be sure the seal is watertight. Label package with name of fruit and date frozen. Freeze; store at 0° F. or below. Plastic bags can also be used for liquid packs.

This same method can be used for blueberries, blackberries and raspberries.

Peaches Packed in Syrup

When Georgia peaches are in season, the kitchen is turned into an assembly line on the day we decide to freeze them. Some of us wash and peel, others pour the syrup and pack the peaches into the containers.

Lyniece usually supervises the operation when we pack peaches in syrup. The syrup should be made ahead of time so it will be ready and cold when you need it. Peaches are best packed in a 40 percent syrup— 3 cups of sugar dissolved in 4 cups of water. Add ½ teaspoon ascorbic acid per pint of peaches. You will need ½ cup of syrup for each pint container of peaches. We usually make it and refrigerate it overnight.

One bushel of fresh peaches will make about 36 pints of frozen peaches. You may want to start with ½ bushel or less in your first attempt. Allow 1 to 1½ pounds fresh peaches for each pint to be frozen.

Select mature peaches that are firm-ripe, with no green color in the skins. Wash them carefully. Pit peaches, and peel them by hand. Peaches can be skinned more quickly if they are dipped first in boiling water, then in cold. Halve the peaches and remove the pits.

Pour ½ cup cold syrup into each pint container. The container should be moisture-vaporproof. Pack peach halves, pit sides down, into container. Add syrup to cover peaches. Leave ½-inch head space at top of wide-mouthed pint containers to allow for expansion during freezing. Syrup should always cover fruit to keep top pieces from changing color and flavor. Remove as many air bubbles as possible from syrup by puncturing them with a dinner knife. Seal and label with the name of fruit and date of freezing. Store containers in coldest part of freezer.

Apples and other fruits can be packed and frozen by this same method.

Figs

We have lovely fig trees at Lovejoy. I keep figs fresh in the refrigerator as long as I can harvest them. But there are always more than we can eat, so we freeze the surplus, usually leaving them whole and unsweetened.

Wash and cut off stems. Pack into containers, leaving head space. Cover with water or not as desired. If water is used, crystalline ascorbic acid or ½ cup lemon juice may be added to retard darkening of light-colored figs—¾ teaspoon to each quart of water. Seal and freeze.

If you want to sweeten figs: Use 35 percent syrup (2½ cups sugar to 4 cups water for 5⅓ cups yield). Add ¾ teaspoon crystalline ascorbic acid or ½ cup lemon juice to each quart of syrup. Pack figs into containers and cover with cold syrup, leaving ½-inch head space. Seal and freeze.

Frozen Tomatoes

Idella North used to can all of her tomatoes, but now she prefers this easy method of freezing. Frozen tomatoes are excellent to use in soups and stews.

Wash and drain tomatoes. Peel and quarter (you can skin the tomatoes first by placing them in boiling water for about half a minute, then dipping them into cold water. The skins will slip off easily). Place in moisture-vaporproof container, seal and quick-freeze.

2

Canning and Pickling

WHEN WE DECIDE to can jellies, jams and pickles, we turn the event into a "community" effort with family and friends. The fun of being together lessens the tasks at hand. We use much of what we can for holiday gifts.

Some helpful hints:

To determine jellying point: Dip a large metal spoon into boiling syrup. Tilt spoon until syrup runs from side. When jellying point is reached, liquid will not flow in a stream but will drop into distinct drops.

Be sure to remember that butters and jams thicken more as they cool. Thickness is difficult to judge when the product is hot.

Don't waste the skins and peelings of apples and peaches when you are freezing whole fruit. They can be cooked along with the less appealing slices when you are preparing jellies and jams.

General preparation of the jars:

Discard jars with cracks and sharp edges on sealing surfaces. Wash the jars and lids in hot soapy water; rinse thoroughly. To sterilize jars and lids, place them in a pan with a rack on the bottom, cover with hot water and bring to a boil. Boil 15 minutes. Keep hot until ready for use by leaving the jars in warm water; or putting them in a warm oven; or leaving them in the dishwasher during the drying process. Be sure to label with the date and contents before storing.

The U.S. Agriculture Department recommends that home canners use pressure canners for meat, poultry and all vegetables except tomatoes. These foods are low in acid and need the high temperature of pressure canning to kill botulism germs as well as organisms that spoil food. However, tomatoes, fruits and pickles can be safely processed in a boiling-water bath as an alternative to pressure canning. But if you add to tomatoes low-acid vegetables such as corn, pepper, okra or celery, you should use a pressure canner.

Pepper Jelly

¾ *cup ground bell pepper*
¼ *cup ground hot pepper*
6 *cups sugar*
1½ *cups white vinegar*

1 *6-ounce bottle liquid pectin*
2 *drops green food coloring (optional)*

Wash peppers and remove seeds. Grind and measure. Add sugar and vinegar and cook until mixture is at a full rolling boil. Cook 1 minute longer, stirring. Remove from heat and add pectin, stirring in well. Let set for a full minute. Pour into hot sterile jars (leave ½-inch head space in jars) and seal. Serve with vegetables and meats, or as an appetizer with cream cheese and crackers. Yield: 3 pints.

Indian Springs Pear Relish

1 *peck (8 quarts) pears*
  bell peppers (3 red, 3 green, or
    4 red, 2 green)
6 *large onions*
5 *cups cider vinegar*

2 *pounds (4 cups) sugar*
1 *teaspoon turmeric*
1 *tablespoon salt*
1 *tablespoon whole pickling spice*

Peel and core pears and, to prevent discoloration, drop pears, as they are peeled, into a solution of 2 tablespoons salt and 2 tablespoons vinegar to 1 gallon cold water. Drain. Coarsely grind pears, peppers and onions. Add vinegar, sugar, turmeric, salt and pickling spice in a small cheesecloth bag. Boil for 30 minutes. Remove pickling-spice bag. Pour into sterilized canning jars and seal, leaving ½-inch head space. Yield: 6 quarts.

Aunt Clyde's Mustard Pickles

1 quart white cabbage	*1 quart green tomatoes*
1 quart onions	*4 large bell peppers*

Chop all the above. Dissolve 1 cup salt in 3 quarts cold water and cover vegetables with this brine. Let stand overnight. Next morning squeeze water out of vegetables and cover them with clear, cold water. Let stand a few minutes then squeeze out water. Make a paste of:

1 quart vinegar	*1 tablespoon butter*
1 cup sugar	*1 teaspoon turmeric*
2 tablespoons dry mustard	*1 red bell pepper*
1 cup flour	
celery and mustard seed	

Begin paste by adding just a little vinegar at a time to the sugar, mustard and flour. When well mixed Aunt Clyde always said, "Add five cents' worth" celery and mustard seed. Also 1 tablespoon butter. Put chopped vegetables in this and let simmer 10 minutes. Stir constantly. Add turmeric. Cut up red pepper before it finishes cooking and add to the mixture "just to make it pretty." Yield: 3 quarts.

Beet Pickles

3 quarts beets	*2 sticks cinnamon*
2 cups sugar	*3½ cups vinegar*
1 tablespoon whole allspice	*1½ cups water*
1½ teaspoon salt	

Wash and drain beets. Leave 2 inches of stems and taproots while cooking (this prevents beets from losing color during cooking). Cover with boiling water and cook until tender. Peel beets, slice and pack into hot jars, leaving ½-inch head space.

Combine rest of ingredients. Simmer 15 minutes. Remove cinnamon. Bring liquid to boiling. Pour while boiling hot over beets, leaving ½-inch head space. Seal. Process for 30 minutes in boiling-water bath. You may omit allspice and cinnamon and use instead 2 tablespoons whole pickling spice. Tie spices in thin cloth and remove from vinegar mixture before pouring into jars. Yield: 6 pints.

Fresh Dill Pickles

1½ gallons cucumbers (2 medium cucumbers for each pint)
4 sprigs of fresh dill to each pint jar
1½ quarts vinegar

1½ quarts water
½ cup salt
¼ teaspoon alum to each pint jar

Wash cucumbers and slice lengthwise. Pack cucumbers in hot sterile pint canning jar with the dill. Set aside. Bring vinegar, water and salt to a boil. Pour into jar to cover cucumbers. Add ¼ teaspoon alum at top of each jar. Leave ½-inch head space. Seal. Yield: 12 pints.

9-Day Pickles

Use only stoneware or glass container for soaking cucumbers. I usually pickle about ½ gallon of small, whole cucumbers at a time in this manner:

First 3 days: Soak cucumbers in salty water (approximately 2 cups salt to 1 gallon water). The water should be salty enough to float an egg in its shell. Make this water mixture fresh each morning, pour over cucumbers while boiling hot. Be sure all are covered.

4th, 5th, 6th days: Soak in alum water (1 tablespoon of alum to 1 gallon of hot water).

7th day: Drain. Measure enough vinegar to cover cucumbers; add an equal amount of sugar. Add 1 tablespoon pickling spice and bring to a boil. Pour over pickles while hot.

8th day: Drain vinegar and sugar mixture off and bring it to a boil. Allow to cool and pour over pickles.

9th day: Pour vinegar and pickles into a large 6-quart pot and boil 5 minutes. Just before putting into jars, add ¼ teaspoon turmeric to each. Put into glass jars or containers. These pickles do not need sealing.

Green Tomato Pickles

1 gallon green tomatoes	*1 tablespoon mustard seed*
6 large onions	*1 tablespoon ground mustard*
½ cup salt	*½ lemon*
1 tablespoon whole black pepper	*3 pods red pepper*
1 tablespoon whole cloves	*3 cups brown sugar*
1 tablespoon whole allspice	*3 cups vinegar*
1 tablespoon crushed celery seed	

Slice the tomatoes and onions thin. Sprinkle ½ cup salt over them and let stand overnight in a crock or enamel vessel. Next morning freshen in cold water for an hour. Tie the pepper, cloves, allspice, celery seed and mustard seed in a cheesecloth bag. Slice the lemon and chop 2 pepper pods very fine. Drain the tomatoes and onions well. Add the brown sugar and all seasonings except 1 red pepper pod to the vinegar, then add the tomatoes and onions. Cook for ½ hour, stirring gently at intervals to prevent burning. Remove spice bag to prevent darkening product. Pack in jars and garnish with slender strips of the remaining red pepper, placing them vertically on the side of jars halfway from top to bottom. Leave ½-inch head space. Adjust lids. Process in boiling-water bath 15 minutes. Yield: about 4 quarts.

Peach Pickles

8 pounds small or medium peaches	*8 two-inch pieces stick cinnamon*
2 tablespoons whole cloves	*2 pounds sugar*
	1 quart vinegar

Use firm ripe peaches (clingstone peaches are best for pickles). Wash and peel peaches. Put cinnamon and cloves in thin cloth (a Talmadge ham bag is perfect!); tie top tightly. Cook together spices, sugar and vinegar for 10 minutes. Add whole peaches, cook slowly until tender, but not broken. Remove from heat and let stand overnight. In the morning remove spices. Drain syrup from peaches; boil syrup rapidly until it begins to thicken. Pack peaches in clean, sterilized jars. Pour hot syrup over peaches, leaving 1½-inch head space. Seal and process for 10 minutes at about 180° F. Yield: about 3 quarts.

Pear Honey

8 cups chopped pears	*1 teaspoon ginger*
1 lemon	*1 large can crushed pineapple*
5 cups sugar	*½ cup water*

Wash, peel, core, and chop pears, or put through food chopper or sausage grinder. Measure pears. Add sliced lemon, sugar, ginger, pineapple, and ½ cup water to pears. Boil slowly until thick, about 45 minutes to 1 hour. Pour boiling hot into hot sterile jars. Seal. Process 15 minutes in hot-water bath.

Fig Preserves

To prepare figs, remove stems, wash and peel (optional) with sharp knife. Use ¾ pound sugar to 1 pound figs. Make syrup, using ½ cup water to 1 cup sugar. When syrup starts boiling, drop figs in a few at a time so the boiling process continues. When the figs are clear (this will take at least ½ hour) put them in jars. Let syrup boil until thick and pour over figs. Seal while hot. (If you are preserving a large quantity, you can use 1 teaspoon cream of tartar for every 5 pounds sugar to keep syrup from sugaring.)

Quick and Easy Strawberry Figs

3 cups peeled figs	*2 small boxes strawberry gelatin*
3 cups sugar	

Wash and peel figs. Mix all ingredients together. Cook for 3 to 5 minutes on high heat. Pour into hot sterile jars and seal. Leave ½-inch head space. (You can use any fruit-flavored gelatin instead of strawberry.) These may be stored on the shelf, but should be chilled in the refrigerator to jell before opening the jar to be used. Yield: 3 pints.

Idella's Watermelon Rind Preserves

11 cups prepared rind
lime water
9 cups sugar
8 cups water

4 lemons, sliced thin
4 sticks cinnamon
4 teaspoons whole cloves

Select melons with thick rinds. Cut off all green skin and pink pulp portions. Use only the white part of the rind, and dice into 1½-inch cubes. Soak in lime water to cover for 3½ hours. To make lime water, use 1 tablespoon unslaked lime to 1 quart water. Freshen rind in 2 or 3 changes of cold water. Cover with water and cook until tender. Drain well.

Make a syrup of sugar, the 8 cups of water, and sliced lemons. Tie into a piece of cheesecloth the cinnamon and cloves, and add to the sugar syrup. Let boil 5 minutes. Add watermelon rind to syrup and cook until transparent. Remove the spices. Take off foam. Let stand overnight or until cold to plump. Stir occasionally.

Pack into hot, sterilized jars to within ½ inch of the top. Seal. Process for 15 minutes in boiling-water bath. When cool, label and store.

Apple Jelly

5 pounds apples (to make 7 cups
apple juice)
5 cups water

1 box "Sure-Jell" (powdered
pectin)
9 cups sugar

Remove blossom and stem ends from *ripe,* tart, juicy apples. Cut in small pieces. Add 5 cups water and simmer, covered, for 10 minutes. Crush with masher and simmer 5 minutes longer. Place in jelly bag (Talmadge ham bags are excellent) and squeeze out juice.

Measure juice into 6- to 8-quart saucepan. (For stiffer jellies use ¼ cup less juice.) Add pectin. Quickly bring mixture to hard boil, stirring occasionally. Add sugar. Bring to full rolling boil (a boil that cannot be stirred down); boil hard 1 minute, stirring constantly. Remove from heat and skim off foam. You may add 4 drops food coloring for a richer color. Pour at once into canning jars or hot jelly glasses, leaving ½-inch head space.

If using jelly glasses, cover jelly immediately with ⅛ inch of melted paraffin. Cool and cover with lids. To tighten the loose-fitting lids, use a square of gingham check or calico under the lid. It adds a decorative flair, besides.

In using canning jars with a 2-piece lid, place lid on jar, screw band on tight and turn jar upside down. Repeat with all jars. When sealed, stand upright.

Blackberry Jelly

If you prefer not to use packaged, powdered or bottled liquid pectin, you can cook the fruit until it jells as in this method:

Wash berries, cover with water and cook until mushy. Strain through cheesecloth (or a Talmadge ham bag) to extract juice. Allow ¾ cup sugar to each cup of juice. If no green berries have been included, add a little lemon juice. Boil hard. When mixture jells, pour into jars. (You will know it is ready when mixture drops in heavy drops from side of spoon.) Cover jars with paraffin after jelly has cooled. Then put on lids.

Apple Butter

2 quarts cooked apple pulp   *2 teaspoons ground cinnamon*
4 cups sugar   *¼ teaspoon ground cloves*

Use apple pulp from preparing apple juice for jelly. Push through sieve. Measure pulp. Add sugar and spices. Cook 15 minutes over medium heat, stirring frequently to prevent sticking. Water can be added if it is too thick. Pour while hot into hot canning jars, leaving ¼-inch head space. Adjust caps. (Since less sugar is used in apple butter than in jelly, it should be processed for 10 minutes in a hot-water bath.) Yield: 5 pints.

Applesauce

Select firm, fresh cooking apples. Wash; peel if desired, core and slice. To each quart of apple slices add ⅓ cup water; cook until tender. Cool and strain; or puree in electric blender. Sweeten to taste with ¼ to ¾ cup sugar for each quart (2 pounds) of sauce. Pack into containers, leaving head space. Seal and freeze.

Tomato Ketchup

At the rate most families consume ketchup, I'm surprised more cooks don't try making it themselves. My recipe calls for a peck of good, ripe tomatoes. For those who might not know, a peck is ¼ of a bushel (or 2 gallons) —or you can just decide it's a "heap" of tomatoes.

1 peck tomatoes	*1 tablespoon black pepper*
2 onions	*2 tablespoons sugar*
2 hot pepper pods	*other spices to taste*
2 tablespoons salt	*1 quart vinegar*

Chop tomatoes, onions and hot peppers. Cook until tender and strain. This makes approximately a gallon of tomato juice. Add salt, pepper, sugar and spices to vinegar and mix with vegetable juice. Cook until thick. If you wish to thicken it more quickly, mix a small amount of flour with cold water and gradually add to tomato mixture. Cook until thick. Seal in bottles. Keep refrigerated.

Vegetables for Soups

If you really feel ambitious, try canning vegetables to have on hand for your homemade soups. A combination of corn, okra and tomatoes makes a tasty blend.

3 cups tomato pulp	*2 teaspoons salt and sugar*
1 cup corn	*mixture to each pint (1 part*
1 cup okra	*salt, 2 parts sugar, well*
	mixed)
	1 tablespoon chopped onion

Scald tomatoes, core and peel, cutting off all green portions. Put through food chopper. Blanch corn on cob 3 minutes, then cut from cob, cutting twice: first, halfway through kernels, then closer to cob for smaller pieces. Blanch okra 1 minute, then dip into cold water, remove and cut into 1/8-inch slices. Measure tomatoes, corn and okra in proportions given above. Bring tomatoes to boil, then add corn and okra; simmer 10 minutes. Put 2 teaspoons salt-sugar mixture and 1 tablespoon chopped onion in empty container. Fill glass jars, leaving 1/2-inch head space; adjust lids and process in steam pressure canner at 10 pounds pressure—quart jars for 45 minutes, pint jars for 40 minutes.

For a larger quantity of soup mixture: Scald and peel 5 quarts of tomatoes. Core and cut into quarters. Combine 5 quarts tomatoes, 2 quarts corn or lima beans, 2 quarts okra, 2 tablespoons salt. Cook to the consistency of thick soup. Fill containers as in recipe above. Adjust lids. Seal. Process in a pressure canner at 10 pounds pressure—quart jars for 45 minutes, pint jars for 40 minutes.

Idella North's Homemade Country Butter

Idella's table is never without homemade butter to go with oven-baked bread and her delicious preserves. She makes it in small quantities and says it's easy. Many grocery stores sell the unprocessed milk you need, so you can do it yourself. This is a quick and easy way to make a small amount of butter. Instead of using the old-time 3- to 4-gallon churn, you can use a ½-gallon glass fruit jar with a tight lid.

Put a pan of fresh non-homogenized milk in a cool place to let the cream rise to the top. It should stand about 8 hours. Skim the cream off into a jar. Fill about ½ full. Set jar aside until the cream has "turned" or clabbered. The time for this depends on the temperature of the cream. In summer it sours more quickly and can be ready in 24 hours, whereas in cooler weather it may take 2 to 4 days. It is important that the clabbered cream be churned when it has just turned. If left too long, the cream will curdle and will not make good butter.

When the cream is ready, shake it for about 20 minutes or until the butter gathers into a ball. Remove the butter and wash in cold water, stirring to remove all the water. Add a pinch of salt, and it is ready to put into a butter dish or a mold—whichever you prefer. This butter can be kept frozen for 2 or 3 months.

The liquid left in the jar after the butter is removed is buttermilk, which can be drunk and is excellent for making biscuits.

FOR MORE INFORMATION

There are many reliable sources for information on food preservation.

The closest and quickest source is your local Cooperative Extension Service. Your county extension agent (home economist) has a variety of free pamphlets that are constantly being updated. Offices are listed in local telephone books under the listings for other county offices.

Other publications available are:

Ball Blue Book Home Canning: Consumer Service Department, Ball Corp., 1509 South Macedonia Ave., Muncie, Ind. 47302—$1.

Ball Freezer Book: same address—75 cents.

Kerr Home Canning & Freezer Book Consumer Products Division, Kerr Manufacturing Corp., Sand Springs, Okla. 74063—$1.

In addition to publications mentioned on pages 224 and 225, the following U.S. Government publications can be purchased from Consumer Product Information Center, Public Documents Distribution Center, Pueblo, Colo. 81009. Make checks payable to Superintendent of Documents.

Freezing Combination Main Dishes, 40 cents.

Storing Vegetables and Fruits at Home, 40 cents.

Home Freezing of Poultry and Poultry Main Dishes, 50 cents.

How to Buy Meat for Your Freezer, 45 cents.

PART VI

After the Dishes Are Done— What Then?

POSSIBLY SOME OF YOU who have flipped through this book (no one ever *reads* a cookbook) have the misconception that I spend a lot of time in the kitchen.

I am a good cook. When I entertain, I do spend time planning and preparing the meal. But I try to practice what I preach—and lately I've been preaching to any number of women's groups that we could all use more time to find ourselves, to develop what talents we might have, to find courage to pursue some ambition or drive we might have put aside while our families were young.

The feeling I have sensed, in speaking to groups of women, is that we are on the threshold of a new self-image. We can be good cooks *and* good company. We can use the kitchen table for preparing a meal *and* for doing our homework for an advanced degree, for helping our children with homework *and* for addressing envelopes to launch a political career, for flower arranging *and* Perhaps even to write the great American novel.

Some of us may need a little encouragement to put forth a new effort. I know I have been more fortunate than most women because I have had a measure of independence and a business interest of my own for such a long period of time. I never felt the need to be liberated.

I try to urge women to get involved in business, politics, or whatever suits their fancy, *now,* before their children are grown and out of the nest. Of course I'm not suggesting that mothers should abandon their children. Like almost everything in life there has to be a proper balance. I've known women who have turned interesting hobbies they pursued while their children were young into lucrative businesses later in life. The early years of childhood are so important that you can't just drop in on your children from time to time. But once you've given them the firm foundation—and while you are doing that—you can be thinking and planning your place in the sun. Qualified women are needed —and women who are qualified should be encouraged by society, and by their husbands and children, to use their brains. If we plan well, we can not only raise a family and provide a loving home, but also eventually, if not always simultaneously, enter the job market. If you wait too long, you'll be in trouble. The life expectancy of women is now 78 years—and it is not all "sweet sixteen," young motherhood and twilight years being entertained by adoring grandchildren. It is, after all, a world of survival. We need to carve out a productive and satisfying place in society. The husband who gives his wife a pat on the back from time to time and protects her almost to the state of outright dependency is doing her a grave disservice.

All of us have different instincts, drives and talents. The object is to find our own. I believe many women are leading the way. A decade or so ago, a Senate wife was considered a "political powder puff," usually a silent partner at political rallies. No longer. Some of the Senate wives I know are real-estate agents, one is an owner of a plant boutique on Capitol Hill, another has been studying, believe it or not, auto mechanics.

Every woman has the potential to become a fully functioning human being in our society. Every woman has the right, indeed the duty, to think of herself, her future and her role in life. Women of today do not want to be regarded as any *more* than any other person, but we are certainly tired, justifiably so, of being regarded as something *less.*

Don't worry about self-confidence. The best way to get that is to get on with what you want to do. Someone put to words what everyone, sooner or later, finds out: "You can never get much of

I like to speak to women about women and business.

anything done unless you go ahead and do it before you are ready." Life is only as busy or as interesting or as productive as you make it.

Aside from meeting new and interesting people, you will find that the additional income will give you a lift—just to buy your husband a present with money that never saw his pocket can be fun. You may also find your husband sharing in some of the household duties out of respect for the time you are spending at work.

A good meal, well cooked and tastefully served, is an accomplishment. It takes talent, too, and I'm not minimizing the women who have made homemaking a career. I'm simply suggesting that for some of us there are alternatives, and someday we may need to use them.

When the children are grown and the dishes are done, what then? It's up to you. Among other things, I wrote a cookbook.

Facts, Charts, Metric Measures, and Other Miscellanea

WHEN YOU'RE IN A METRIC JAM

Since we will all be involved with metric measurements in the near future, here is a useful explanation which can serve as our primer to get us through the learning period.

METRIC MEASURES ON NUTRITION LABELS*

One of the first things consumers will notice about the new nutrition information food labels is that metric units are used throughout. These are the measuring units used in most of the world.

The metric system is based on the decimal system of numbers, which involves multiples of 10. Thus, it is very easy to go from small units to large, or vice versa, by simply moving decimal points.

The Food and Drug Administration prescribed the metric system for nutrition labels because the unit we are most accustomed to, the ounce, is too large to describe conveniently the amounts of nutrients in foods. For instance, 1 gram is about equal to the weight of a paper clip. If a food contains 9 grams of protein, then, expressing this in our customary terms, it would be 9/28 ounce. This is just an example of how

* U.S. Department of Health, Education, and Welfare, Public Health Service, Food and Drug Administration, 5600 Fishers Lane, Rockville, Md. 20852. DHEW Publication No. (FDA) 73-2041.

244

customary measurements used for food composition would not only be very small but appear as confusing fractions.

The basic metric units that consumers will see on nutrition labels are grams (units of mass or weight) and liters (units of volume). Metric units of volume may appear in the serving size for liquid foods as well as in the container's net volume. The upper portion of the label will use metric units in weight as grams for protein, carbohydrate, and fat in a serving of food.

The lower portion of the nutrition information panel gives the *percentage* of the U.S. Recommended Daily Allowances of protein, vitamins and minerals in a serving, and does not require any understanding of the metric system.

It may help to memorize these approximate equivalencies:

> One ounce = 28 grams
> Three and one-half ounces = 100 grams
> Eight ounces = 227 grams
> One pound = 454 grams

Once the basic unit is determined, whether grams or liters in the metric system, other multiples are built on it with suitable prefixes. Whenever the prefix "kilo" precedes a unit, it is 1,000 times that unit. One kilogram equals 1,000 grams, for example.

Similarly, the prefix "milli" indicates one-thousandth and "micro" one-millionth of the basic unit. A milligram is one-thousandth of a gram.

Thus:

> 1 kilogram = 1,000 grams
> 1 gram = 1,000 milligrams
> 1 milligram = 1,000 micrograms

To convert the metric system into the system to which Americans are more accustomed:

> 1 kilogram = 2.2 pounds
> 1 pound = 454 grams
> 1 ounce = 28 grams

The other basic unit of metric measurement besides the gram that will be found on nutrition labels is the liter, used to measure volume.

> A liter is a little larger than a quart.
> 1 kiloliter = 1,000 liters
> 1 liter = 1,000 milliliters

To translate this system into the one currently used in the United States:

> 1 gallon = 3.79 liters
> 1 quart = .95 liters
>   or 950 milliliters
> 1 pint = .48 liters
>   or 480 milliliters
> 1 cup (8 fluid ounces) = .24 liters
>   or 240 milliliters
> 1 tablespoon = 15 milliliters
> 1 teaspoon = 5 milliliters

Remember the saying "A pint is a pound, the world around"? Well, this is a rough approximation based on a volume-weight relationship of water. A pint of food that contains more fat than water will weigh less than a pound.

These same relationships of volume to weight and fat to water carry through to the metric system. Here is a new twist to an old saying to help you remember that pints and liters are volume measurements and pounds and kilograms are weight:

> *A pint is a pound the world around, but*
> *A liter is a kilogram*
> *When you're in a metric jam.*

STANDARD WEIGHTS, MEASURES AND EQUIVALENTS

3 teaspoons = 1 tablespoon
2 tablespoons = 1 liquid ounce
4 tablespoons = ¼ cup
16 tablespoons = 1 cup
2 cups = 1 pint
2 pints = 1 quart
4 quarts = 1 gallon
8 quarts = 1 peck
4 pecks = 1 bushel
16 ounces = 1 pound
4 cups flour = 1 pound
3 cups cornmeal = 1 pound
2 cups granulated sugar = 1 pound
3½ cups confectioner's sugar (sifted) = 1 pound
2¼ cups brown sugar (firmly packed) = 1 pound
8 to 10 egg whites = 1 cup
13 to 14 egg yolks = 1 cup

2 cups butter = 1 pound
4 tablespoons flour = 1 ounce
1 ounce chocolate = ⅓ cup cocoa
1 cup raisins = 6 ounces
1 pound walnuts or pecans in shell = ½ pound shelled
1 cup walnuts shelled = ¼ pound
1 cup pecans shelled = ⅓ pound
1 cup almonds shelled = ¼ pound
⅓ cup blanched, chopped almonds = 1 ounce
1 small square compressed yeast = 1 package dry granular yeast
1 lemon (juice) = 2½ to 3½ tablespoons
1 orange (juice) = 5 to 6 tablespoons

Fruits and Vegetables

1 bushel plums = 50 pounds
1 bushel pears = 48 pounds
1 bushel peaches = 48 pounds
1 bushel apples = 44 pounds
1 bushel tomatoes = 50 pounds

1 peck potatoes = 15 pounds
1 peck peas in pods = 7½ pounds
1 peck spinach = 3½ to 4 pounds

TABLES ON PIG COOKERY

ROASTING AT 300° F.-350° F.* OVEN TEMPERATURE

Cut	Approx. Weight	Meat Thermometer Reading	Approx. Cooking Time**
FRESH	Pounds	Degrees F.	Min. Per Lb.
Loin			
Center	3 to 5	170° F.	30 to 35
Half	5 to 7	170° F.	35 to 40
End	3 to 4	170° F.	40 to 45
Roll	3 to 5	170° F.	35 to 40
Boneless Top	2 to 4	170° F.	30 to 35
Crown	4 to 6	170° F.	35 to 40
Picnic Shoulder			
Bone-in	5 to 8	170° F.	30 to 35
Rolled	3 to 5	170° F.	35 to 40
Boston Shoulder	4 to 6	170° F.	40 to 45
Leg (fresh ham)			
Whole (bone in)	12 to 16	170° F.	22 to 26
Whole (boneless)	10 to 14	170° F.	24 to 28
Half (bone-in)	5 to 8	170° F.	35 to 40
Tenderloin	½ to 1		45 to 60
Back Ribs		Cooked	1½ to 2½ hrs.
Country-style		Well	
Backbones		Done	1½ to 2½ hrs.
Spareribs			1½ to 2½ hrs.
Pork Loaf	2		1¾ hrs.

SMOKED	Pounds	Degrees F.	Min. Per Lb.
Ham			
(cook-before-eating)			
Whole	10 to 14	160° F.	18 to 20
Half	5 to 7	160° F.	22 to 25
Shank Portion	3 to 4	160° F.	35 to 40
Butt Portion	3 to 4	160° F.	35 to 40
Ham (fully-cooked)***			
Half	5 to 7	140° F.	18 to 24
Loin	3 to 5	160° F.	25 to 30
Picnic Shoulder			
(cook-before-eating)	5 to 8	170° F.	30 to 35
Picnic Shoulder			
(fully-cooked)	5 to 8	140° F.	25 to 30
Shoulder Roll (butt)	2 to 4	170° F.	35 to 40
Canadian-style Bacon	2 to 4	160° F.	35 to 40
Ham Kabobs	1" to 1½"		45 to 60
	cubes		
Ham Loaf	2	160° F.	1½ hrs.
Ham Patties	1" thick	160° F.	45 to 60

*325° F. to 350° F. oven temperature is recommended for fres pork and 300° F. to 325° F. oven temperature for smoked por
**Based on meat taken directly from the refrigerator.
***Heat "fully-cooked" whole hams to 140° F. internal temperatur Allow 15 to 18 minutes per pound for heating.

BROILING AT MODERATE TEMPERATURE

Cut	Approx. Thickness	Approx. Total Cooking Time
SMOKED		Minutes
Ham Slice	½ inch	10 to 12
Ham Slice	1 inch	16 to 20
Loin Chops	½ to ¾ inch	15 to 20
Canadian-style Bacon		
Sliced	¼ inch	6 to 8
Sliced	½ inch	8 to 10
Bacon		4 to 5
Ham Patties	1 inch	16 to 20
FRESH		
Rib or Loin Chops	¾ to 1 inch	20 to 25
Shoulder Steaks	½ to ¾ inch	20 to 22
Patties	1 inch	20 to 25
Pork Kabobs	1½ x 1½ x ¾ to	
	1 inch	22 to 25

BRAISING

Cut	Approx. Weight or Thickness	Approx. Total Cooking Time
Chops, Fresh	¾ to 1½ inches	45 to 60 min.

Spareribs	2 to 3 pounds	1½ hrs.
Backribs		1½ to 2 hrs.
Country-style Backbones		1½ to 2 hrs.
Tenderloin		
Whole	¾ to 1 pound	45 to 60 min.
Fillets	½ inch	30 min.
Shoulder Steaks	¾ inch	45 to 60 min.
Cubes	1 to 1¼ inches	45 to 60 min.

COOKING IN LIQUID

Cut	Approx. Weight	Total Cooking Time
SMOKED	Pounds	Hours
Ham (old style and		
country cured)		
Large	12 to 16	4½ to 5
Small	10 to 12	4½ to 5
Half	5 to 8	3 to 4
Picnic Shoulder	5 to 8	3½ to 4
Shoulder Roll	2 to 4	1½ to 1¾
Hocks		2 to 2½
FRESH		
Spareribs		2 to 2½
Country-style Backbones		2 to 2½
Hocks		2½ to 3

NATIONAL PORK PRODUCERS COUNCII

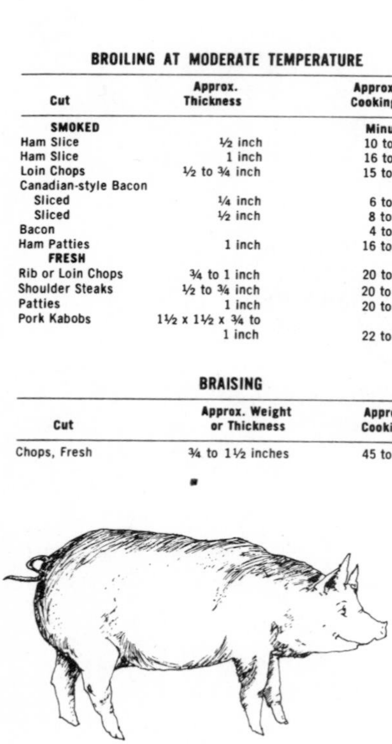

PORK CHART

RETAIL CUTS OF PORK — WHERE THEY COME FROM AND HOW TO COOK THEM

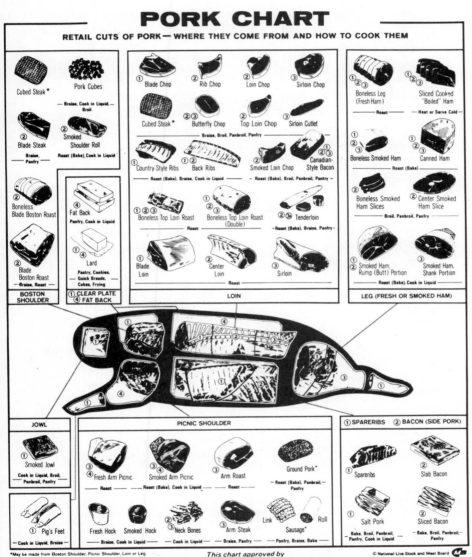

BOSTON SHOULDER

Cubed Steak *

Pork Cubes
— Braise, Cook in Liquid, Broil —

② Blade Steak
Braise, Panfry

Smoked Shoulder Roll
Roast (Bake), Cook in Liquid

② Boneless Blade Boston Roast

② Blade Boston Roast
— Braise, Roast —

① CLEAR PLATE ④ FAT BACK

④ Fat Back
Panfry, Cook in Liquid

④ Lard
Pastry, Cookies, Quick Breads, Cakes, Frying

LOIN

① Blade Chop
② Rib Chop
② Loin Chop
③ Sirloin Chop

Cubed Steak *
②③ Butterfly Chop
Top Loin Chop
③ Sirloin Cutlet
— Braise, Broil, Panbroil, Panfry —

① Country-Style Ribs
①② Back Ribs
Smoked Loin Chop
②③ Canadian-Style Bacon
— Roast (Bake), Braise, Cook in Liquid — — Roast (Bake), Broil, Panbroil, Panfry —

①②③ Boneless Top Loin Roast
①②③ Boneless Top Loin Roast (Double)
②③ Tenderloin
— Roast — — Roast (Bake), Braise, Panfry —

① Blade Loin
② Center Loin
③ Sirloin
— Roast —

LEG (FRESH OR SMOKED HAM)

①②③ Boneless Leg (Fresh Ham)
①②③ Sliced Cooked "Boiled" Ham
— Roast — — Heat or Serve Cold —

①②③ Boneless Smoked Ham
①②③ Canned Ham
— Roast (Bake) —

① Boneless Smoked Ham Slices
② Center Smoked Ham Slice
— Broil, Panbroil, Panfry —

② Smoked Ham, Rump (Butt) Portion
③ Smoked Ham, Shank Portion
— Roast (Bake), Cook in Liquid —

JOWL

① Smoked Jowl
Cook in Liquid, Broil, Panbroil, Panfry

① Pig's Feet
— Cook in Liquid, Braise —

PICNIC SHOULDER

③ Fresh Arm Picnic
Roast
③ Smoked Arm Picnic
— Roast (Bake), Cook in Liquid —
Arm Roast
Roast
Ground Pork*
— Roast (Bake), Panbroil, Panfry —

Fresh Hock
Smoked Hock
— Braise, Cook in Liquid — — Cook in Liquid —
② Neck Bones
③ Arm Steak
— Braise, Panfry —
Link
Sausage*
— Panfry, Braise, Bake —
Roll

① SPARERIBS ② BACON (SIDE PORK)

① Spareribs
Slab Bacon

① Salt Pork
② Sliced Bacon
— Bake, Broil, Panbroil, Pantry, Cook in Liquid — — Bake, Broil, Panbroil, Panfry —

*May be made from Boston Shoulder, Picnic Shoulder, Loin or Leg.

© National Live Stock and Meat Board

This chart approved by
National Live Stock and Meat Board

TIPS*

Because cooking time varies with intensity of heat produced, a pork Roast cooked on an outdoor rotisserie may require a longer time to cook on a breezy day.

Pork may be floured before browning, if desired. Floured meats brown better than unfloured meats.

Many cuts of pork can be braised without added liquid. Steam from meat juices provides enough moisture.

If you add a liquid, such as water or tomato juice, use just enough to keep meat from scorching.

Cured, smoked pork is especially tasty when cooked with potatoes, carrots, green beans, or cabbage. Add vegetables just long enough before the meat is tender to cook them.

If the meat is to be served cold, it will be more flavorful and juicy if it is chilled in the liquid in which it was cooked.

Making gravy: For thin gravy use 1 tablespoon of flour to each cup of liquid; for a medium-thick gravy, use 2 tablespoons of flour. If drippings are scarce or meat broth is weakly flavored, add a bouillon cube or a little meat extract to the liquid.

* From "Pork in Family Meals, a Guide for Consumers," U.S. Government Printing Office, 1975, U.S. Dept. of Agriculture, Home and Garden Bulletin No. 160.

POULTRY CHART

This timetable is based on chilled or completely thawed poultry placed in a preheated oven. Unstuffed poultry may require slightly less than quoted times. For best results, use a meat thermometer:

Internal temperature of poultry when done—180–185° F.
Internal temperature of stuffing when done—165° F.

POULTRY		Ready-to-cook weight	Approx. roasting time at 325°F.
CHICKEN	*broilers or fryers*	1½ to 2½ lbs.	1 to 2 hours
DUCK		4 to 6 lbs.	2 to 3 hours
GOOSE		6 to 12 lbs.	3 to 4½ hours
ROCK CORNISH GAME HEN		About 18 oz.	1¼ hours at 350°F.
TURKEY	*hens toms*	6 to 8 lbs.	3 to 3½ hours
		8 to 12 lbs.	3½ to 4½ hours
		12 to 16 lbs.	4½ to 5½ hours
		16 to 20 lbs.	5½ to 6½ hours
		20 to 24 lbs.	6½ to 7 hours
	halves, or quarters	3 to 8 lbs.	2 to 3 hours
		8 to 12 lbs.	3 to 4 hours

Note: Unstuffed turkeys require about ½ hour less roasting time.

SEASONING VEGETABLES
WITH
SPICES AND HERBS

VEGETABLE	SPICE OR HERB[1]
Asparagus	Mustard seed, sesame seed, or tarragon.
Beans, lima	Marjoram, oregano, sage, savory, tarragon, or thyme.
Beans, snap	Basil, dill, marjoram, mint, mustard seed, oregano, savory, tarragon, or thyme.
Beets	Allspice, bay leaves, caraway seed, cloves, dill, ginger, mustard seed, savory, or thyme.
Broccoli	Caraway seed, dill, mustard seed, or tarragon.
Brussels sprouts	Basil, caraway seed, dill, mustard seed, sage, or thyme.
Cabbage	Caraway seed, celery seed, dill, mint, mustard seed, nutmeg, savory, or tarragon.
Carrots	Allspice, bay leaves, caraway seed, dill, fennel, ginger, mace, marjoram, mint, nutmeg, or thyme.
Cauliflower	Caraway seed, celery salt, dill, mace, or tarragon.
Cucumbers	Basil, dill, mint, or tarragon.
Eggplant	Marjoram or oregano.
Onions	Caraway seed, mustard seed, nutmeg, oregano, sage, or thyme.
Peas	Basil, dill, marjoram, mint, oregano, poppy seed, rosemary, sage, or savory.
Potatoes	Basil, bay leaves, caraway seed, celery seed, dill, chives, mustard seed, oregano, poppy seed, or thyme.
Salad greens	Basil, chives, dill, or tarragon.
Spinach	Basil, mace, marjoram, nutmeg, or oregano.

[1] Pepper and parsley may be added to any of the above vegetables. Curry powder is good with creamed vegetables.

VEGETABLE (*cont.*)	SPICE OR HERB (*cont.*)
SQUASH	Allspice, basil, cinnamon, cloves, fennel, ginger, mustard seed, nutmeg, or rosemary.
SWEET POTATOES	Allspice, cardamom, cinnamon, cloves, or nutmeg.
TOMATOES	Basil, bay leaves, celery seed, oregano, sage, sesame seed, tarragon, or thyme.

From U.S. Department of Agriculture's Home and Garden Bulletin No. 105, "Vegetables in Family Meals."

Abraham Lincoln said to members of his bodyguard who protested their assignment to Washington when they wanted to be at the front:

"You boys remind me of a farmer friend of mine in Illinois, who said he could never understand why the Lord put the curl in a pig's tail. It never seemed to him to be either useful or ornamental, but he reckoned that the Almighty knew what he was doing when he put it there."

—*from* McBride, Lincoln's Body Guard, *Indiana Historical Society, Publications, No. 5, 1915.*

ACKNOWLEDGMENTS

COOKING THIS BOOK took more than a mixture of Jean, Carolyn and me. The secret ingredients included family and friends who were willing to share their time and their recipes, old-time and timely. Some tasted and tested, others read and reread the recipes, and some just cheered us on. We would like to acknowledge them:

Elena Amos, Martha Bauman, Gwen and Jim Bentley, Mary Pat Begeman, Kitty Brewster, Aunt Louise Cannon, C. L. Chapman, William P. Clark, Senate Dining Room Chef Antonio Coia, Eunice Davis, Flo Davis, Sue Duncan, Aunt Lelia Garden, Yolande Gwin, White House Chef Henry Haller, Louise Hastings, 'Cile Kelly, Blanche Ledford, Anita Maddox, Ilse Mainzer, Aunt Clyde McKenzie, Ellie Montgomery, Idella North, Barbara Scott, Aunt Lillie Shingler, Mama Shingler, Lyniece Talmadge, Mother Talmadge, Jean Thwaite, Lillian Watt, Liz Wharton, Aileen Wieland, Annie Wilson and Ruby Wimberly.

Among those who cheered us on were Liz Carpenter, Don Carter, J. Felton Covington, Jr., Caroline and Don Harkleroad, and Joe Robitscher.

Mountains of typing and collating were done by Carol Kilroy in Atlanta, for careful correcting by Gerry Sachs and design and layout by Eve Metz in New York. And we owe our editor at Simon and Schuster, Larry Ashmead, and his assistant, Richie Barker, a metric ton of thanks for editorial guidance and for simply surviving.

Index of Recipes

(A General Index begins on page 268)

General Index

(An Index of Recipes begins on page 257)